Actions do
speak louder!
John Budesma

ACTIONS SPEAK
LOUDER

ACTIONS SPEAK LOUDER

111 Ways to TURN UP the Volume

JOHN C. BRIDGMAN

10   9   8   7   6   5   4   3   2   1

Library of Congress Cataloging-in-Publication Data

Bridgman, John C. 1937–
    Actions Speak Louder : 111 Ways to Turn Up the Volume
    ISBN 978-0-615-32315-2
    Self help, motivational

Published by Bridgman Consulting
3610 Glenwood Avenue
Wichita Falls, Texas 76308
940-867-2945
www.actionsspeaklouderbook.com

Other Books by the Author
    Time Out ... It's Your Call
    Texas Two-Step Diet (with Amy D. Bradshaw)

Book and cover design by Isabel Lasater Hernandez
Editing by Dixie L. Nixon

Printed in the United States of America by Thomson-Shore

Dedication and Acknowledgments

I would like to dedicate this book to my mother, Neva Bridgman Wise, and to my dear, loving wife and best friend, Gretchen. Both have lived their lives as models of "actions speak louder than words." They are totally unselfish, always thinking of others first and doing the right things for the right reasons.

My thanks to Gretchen for her advice, analysis and contributions to the content and clarity of the articles. I would also like to thank Dixie Nixon for her skillful editing and Isabel Lasater Hernandez for the design of the book and the cover.

Contents

Foreword

If he didn't do so many other things so well, John Bridgman would make a great life coach—which, in his previous works (*Time Out … It's Your Call* and *The Texas Two-Step Diet*) he has been. With his newest work, *Actions Speak Louder: 111 Ways to Turn up the Volume,* Coach Bridgman has the right strategy to coach his new team of readers into winners. Almost all of us can discern that we need to get from A to Z (I need to drop 40 pounds; I need to fix my marriage; I need to do better on my job; I need to cross the goal line). The problem is that a lot of us don't know how to get from A to B and then from B to C (or, to continue the coaching analogy, from the 20- to the 25- to the 30-yard line). With his engineer's acumen, his affable writing style, and his deep faith, John offers wise and gentle counsel on how to succeed in everything from impressing the boss to restoring a relationship to making life more worth living, one action at a time. There's not an ounce of fluff in this book, and certainly no wooly-headed New Age metaphysics—just good, solid, practical, time-tested wisdom. *Actions Speak Louder* has been a blessing to me already; the longer I savor its wisdom, the more I anticipate the blessings abounding, one at a time.

Dr. David B. Hartman, Jr.
Senior Minister, First Christian Church
Wichita Falls, Texas

Action Categories

Career
Actions that help to improve performance in order to become a more productive employee or manager; steps to take in finding employment.

Caring
Actions that emphasize concern and empathy for others.

Celebrating
Actions concerned with joy, remembrance, special occasions and holidays that are important events in our lives.

Coaching
Actions that stress leading, motivating, instructing and training in achieving goals or improving performance.

Committing
Actions that apply to completing tasks on time or taking a particular course of action for a specific objective.

Communicating
Actions that focus on a two-way process wherein listening is as important as speaking; guidance in written and oral communication.

Country
Actions that highlight our country's strengths and suggest areas for improvement; emphasis on patriotism.

Cultivate Character
Actions that focus on improving or strengthening moral or ethical character.

Introduction

The 111 actions in this book first appeared as my weekly articles in the Wichita Falls *Times Record News*. They have been rewritten to focus on the importance of taking action in various important areas of our lives.

The publisher and editor of the *Times Record News* generously approved my use of these articles for the book. I would like to express my deep appreciation for their approval and their support of the project.

Actions do speak louder than words. We respect and admire those who demonstrate their character—who they really are—by their actions, not by what they write or say.

Too often we hear speakers imply, "Do as I say, not as I do." Wouldn't it be better if they just talked about those things they take pride in doing all the time? The speakers' messages would be so much more powerful and motivational if we knew they truly practiced what they preached.

The actions in *Actions Speak Louder* could be incorporated into all facets of one's life. The goal of the book is to provide ideas and suggestions to help you have a more rewarding and meaningful life. The driving force in the book is to take positive actions that make sense to you—not just to read the words and say, "that sounds nice."

The actions are classified under eight categories: Career; Caring; Communicating; Celebrating; Coaching; Committing; Country; and Cultivate Character. These categories are defined on the previous page and preceding the Index at the back of the book. You will find the actions listed in the Index under the appropriate categories. I hope you will find the categories of most interest to you and the corresponding actions that you would like to read—those that say "read me first."

"The Written Word"

Is the word written if it is not read?
Is the word written if it is not understood?

Is the word written if it is not believed?
Is the word written if there is no action?
If the word is read, understood and believed
and yet there is no action ...
Is the word written?
When the word is read, understood and believed
and there is action ...
There is love

It is my hope that some of these 111 actions will bring joy and meaningful results into your lives—and that *there is love* with all of them.

Write Yourself a Letter

It's a powerful, personal way to set your goals.

Any time of year is a good time to be setting goals. When you are beginning the goal-setting process, take time to reflect on the past year, to give thanks for all that went well and to ask for help in those areas that didn't go so well. Make notes to remind yourself of all that happened that was especially meaningful to you.

Why not just sit right down and write yourself a letter? This is an important *Actions Speak Louder* way to turn up the volume in your life. Write yourself a personal, honest letter addressed to you and to be read only by you. Tell yourself what you want to accomplish during the next twelve months. Now is the time to list goals that are most important to you in achieving increased happiness and improved long-term health. There are probably other areas that you would want to include in this goal-setting process.

You might ask, "Why write a letter?" The answer: because writing is powerful. Writing will make your thoughts clearer and better organized, and when you're finished, you'll have a written record that you can use to remind yourself of your goals.

Write It Down

- Do the right things consistently, write them down, and in time you will get the right results.
- Keep a little notebook with you at all times.
- Take notes when you hear something you want to remember.
- Even for little decisions, make lists of pros and cons. Write down what you know and what you don't know.
- Take time to put your most important thoughts in writing.

Several days after writing your letter to yourself, reread it and see if you are serious about all of your goals. Are your goals attainable? Have you listed them in order of importance to you? Are these goals high-priority in your life?

Another *Actions Speak Louder* way will be setting priorities. Please know that it is okay to change your letter to yourself or even write a new one ... only you will know. After reading the action on setting priorities, you might consider setting different goals or modifying the ones you already have.

Consider keeping the letter to yourself in a visible place where you will regularly see what was written. This will be a reminder of the goals you have set. Seeing the letter will also help you to stay focused on your top priorities. Down the road, it might even be a motivator to make positive adjustments with existing or new goals.

Write an honest to goodness letter (not an e-mail) to an old friend whom you haven't heard from recently.

Establish Priorities

Make a list of what you hope to accomplish this year.

Most corporations and organizations have a long-range plan. It may be a three- or five-year plan, or sometimes even longer.

Many in business believe spending time on long-range planning is not productive. That's probably because not enough serious and creative effort goes into the process. Except for the current year, the plans are usually forgotten until the next year when it has to be done again.

What can we learn from this? What about you? Are you spending serious, creative time on your own long-range lifetime plan? Or are you basically drifting day to day in business and personal routines? Is this important?

Of course it is. Just think about it. Shouldn't your long-range, lifetime plan warrant serious and creative effort? What could be more important? You and your family deserve this to be done in a professional way on a regular basis. You don't need a professional to do this ... you just need to do it.

What are your personal priorities? Do you and your spouse have mutually agreed-upon priorities in your life? Do you talk about priorities? If you can't list them clearly, how can you expect to make the most of your life?

This *Actions Speak Louder* way is to establish your priorities. The action is to list what is important to you. Begin this process by writing down at least the top five priorities in your personal life today—the things you want most to focus on during the next year as part of your lifetime plan.

Next, write down at least the top five priorities in your work life. Same thing: What is it that you want most to do? Be honest.

Now, over the next week, make a record of how you spend your time. You can make your own time categories. If you don't want to be this structured, you can just think about how you are spending your time. Don't be surprised if your time-spent analysis is quite different from what you had expected.

Doing this little exercise may seem a waste of time, and maybe for you it will be. However, if it is not, the benefits of refocusing time on higher-priority actions can be huge for you, your family and your job.

Is there a difference between your top priorities and the way you spend your time? Should you consider making adjustments in your daily life? Can dedication, determination and desire help you to establish actions to focus on your priorities?

Take Control of Your Time

- Say no sometimes. Your time is limited. Remember that if you say yes to one thing, you'll probably have to say no to something else.
- Do it now. That way you won't forget.
- Today, promise yourself to eliminate two to three of your regular habits that are a waste of time. Put your commitment in writing.
- Believe that time management is very important. If you have taken a time-management course, review those actions you should be taking each day. If you have not taken such a course, consider doing so.
- Be conscientious about doing first things first.

Plan to have a good and productive day today.

CULTIVATE CHARACTER

Ask the Right Questions

When making decisions, bounce ideas off those whom you trust.

There are many important times during one's life when major decisions need to be made. There are also times when major decisions should be made, but are simply put off. Or maybe they were made, but not as soon as they should have been. This happens to all of us for many different reasons. One of these is procrastination, which is a powerful enemy.

Examples of these procrastinated decisions could be starting a savings or IRA account, stopping smoking, losing weight, getting into shape, volunteer work, church involvement, changing jobs, or going back to school. It could be making the decision to spend more time with family and friends and less time working. Or how about actually establishing real priorities in life?

There are many others. Have you had any of these procrastinated decisions in the past? Or do you have decisions now that deserve attention, and that you just haven't gotten around to dealing with? Why is that? Sometimes it is simply easier to do nothing. This is one of the ways procrastination acts as our enemy. When making decisions, we need friends, not enemies.

Ask yourself if there is a need for making significant changes in your life. Ask those close to you, including your spouse. Ask questions and listen for the right answers.

Questions and Answers

- Ask the right questions for the right reasons.
- Don't ask questions if you're not prepared for the answer.
- Don't answer questions if the person asking is not prepared for the answer.
- Not all questions require an answer. Be kind and considerate when asking or answering.
- Be a good listener. What is the real reason for the question?

If you determine that there are multiple decisions to be made, or at least more than one, decide which is most important to your health and happiness and the health and happiness of your family. Tackle the most important decisions first. It is hard to understand why little decisions are sometimes much harder to make than major decisions. Recognize that this might be the situation facing you. Decide to concentrate on the big decisions before addressing the little ones. Or just devote a little time and effort on little decisions.

Is there someone you haven't thanked properly? If so, take this opportunity to do it today.

CULTIVATE CHARACTER

Words, Words, Words

We want more than words, words, words.

It seems that we are spending so much time these days listening to words, words, words. Not only in political talks where we hear words, words, words, but also all day long we are with people who want to talk, talk and talk more. And quite often, in political talks as well as in everyday conversations, the words don't go together to make much sense. Some people probably just want to talk to hear themselves talk.

Just words? Who is it who keeps saying "just words"? Can you recall a time when someone was giving a speech, a sermon, or just talking, when you thought to yourself, "That really sounded great. Really wonderful words, but what did he or she say? What was the message"?

People can be put into categories based on their talking habits. Where do you think you fit? Here are a few of these categories:

Me first—Some are always the first to talk, first to answer a question, first to offer an opinion. Someone has to be first, but why does it always have to be the same person?

Likes to talk—These are the ones who simply like to hear themselves talk. There are those who have to add their words, words, words to every discussion. Unfortunately, most committees have one of these members, and some very unproductive committees may have two or three of the "likes to talk" members.

I and me—These are the ones who always direct the conversation to talking about themselves.

Waits until asked—These are the ones who don't volunteer information—they have to be asked to participate, to share their ideas and opinions. Don't forget them.

Listener—Listens first, second, third and then comments. These are the ones who are quiet, apparently listening all the time, and then only speaking when the time is right. Usually when they do speak, people listen to what they have to say.

Organizer—This is the person who is able and willing to summarize and organize by putting the different thoughts and comments in an order of importance or priority. This is the one who is good at planning the work.

Doer—This is the one who wants to start immediately doing something. They are ahead of "planning the work and working the plan." They just want to do it.

One-upper—This is the person who always has to one-up you with something that is bigger or better. No matter what you have done, they have done more. A one-upper is quite often a big name-dropper.

Exaggerator—This person tends to bend the truth with exaggerations to the point that you wonder what is true and what is not. Sometimes this person even exaggerates the exaggeration, and this takes some real talent.

How important are words? Do we want to be thought of as being in one or more of these talking categories, and if so, which ones? Would this mean making some changes? Oliver Wendell Holmes said, "Speak clearly, if you speak at all, carve every word before you let it fall."

Today or tomorrow, let's do an experiment with just words, talking habits and talking categories. Let's commit to doing the following for one full day:

Speaking and Listening Experiment

- Be a good listener. See how long you can listen without talking.
- In a group discussion, either be the last one to speak or don't speak at all unless someone asks for your opinion.
- When you don't know what to say—say nothing.
- Refrain from any remarks that could be construed as being hurtful or that could sound hurtful. Focus only on words that are encouraging and positive.

When thinking about these four experimental tips, consider that "ignorance is always eager to speak." Wisdom dictates that the best time to hold your tongue is when you feel as if you "just have to say something." Some people speak from experience; others, from experience, don't speak. That's because they've learned better.

After the day's experiment is over, evaluate how you feel and what you've learned. What about tomorrow?

If you are given the opportunity to form a committee, choose your members carefully to get the right balance. It is difficult to do because there are friendships, office or organizational politics, people's feelings and positions to consider. Sometimes it is the right thing to choose the wrong person. Best advice may be to focus on being kind and considerate.

Become a good listener and see what all you learn.

CARING

Help and Be Helped

Dedication and determination are key steps to health and happiness.

An important action is to ask for help in almost all situations. It just makes good, logical sense to ask for help when faced with problems, difficult situations or hard decisions. There aren't many good reasons for feeling you have to go it alone.

Many times it will require real dedication and determination for actions to speak louder. I believe being dedicated, with determination, in helping others and asking for help can positively lead to increased happiness. There are a few quotations that provide some answers in our search for happiness:

Happiness is a by-product of an effort to make someone else happy.
Gretta Brooker Palmer

The Constitution only guarantees the American people the right to pursue happiness. You have to catch it yourself. Benjamin Franklin

If you want others to be happy, practice compassion. If you want to be happy, practice compassion. Dalai Lama

It seems clear that we cannot be happy if those whom we love and spend time with are not happy. And we are happy when our loved ones and others around us are happy. So, is it obvious that we should focus on helping others and making others happy, especially those whom we love? Should this be a priority, a high priority? The answer is yes.

With this observation in mind, consider the following *Actions Speak Louder* tips for happiness:

Help and Be Helped

- Call an old friend today just to say hello.
- Do something special for your spouse, a friend or someone in your family.
- Do a little act of kindness for a stranger.
- Thank someone whom you should have thanked before.
- Tell someone you're sorry for something you did in the past.
- Help someone—in the right way for the right reason.
- Help someone anonymously.
- Write an honest to goodness letter (not an e-mail) to an old friend whom you haven't heard from recently.

It has been said that everyone has special gifts, talents and interests. It is okay not to have all of them, because we need to share and accept sharing from others. Use the help. Help can come from any number of people and often from those you would least expect.

Enjoy and have fun helping others.

COMMITTING

Making It Happen

Happiness is difficult to define.

We all want good health and happiness for ourselves, our families and those whom we love. Obviously, we want to do those things that will contribute to happiness and health and avoid the things that lead to unhappiness, or that will hurt our health. This should be a high priority for us, but are we fully committed to it?

Happiness

Happiness is complicated because it's difficult to define and is different for most people. What makes one person happy does not necessarily make another happy. Analyzing people who always seem to be happy does lead us to the conclusion that happiness comes with making others happy—when those around us are happy, we are happy.

Happiness also comes with success—your success and the success of those whom you love. Defining success is also rather complicated. Like happiness, success for one is not success for another.

The following is an example of a successful and happy man giving advice to others about being successful and happy:

Mark Pueter was the commencement speaker a few years ago at the spring graduation ceremony at Midwestern State University in Wichita Falls, Texas. He said nobody remembers the commencement speaker or what was said. This probably is true for most graduations. At the end of his talk, he said that for success and happiness, he wanted the graduates to remember just two things (actually, I think his talk was addressed to all of us in attendance): "Number one is to call your mother frequently." He repeated this: "Call your mother frequently; the second is to spend time with people you love."

This is great advice. I would add just one thing to this for success and happiness, and that is to stay focused. Focus on your priorities.

Health

Now about health: For something so very important to our happiness, shouldn't we focus on healthy eating and healthy living? Using *Actions Speak Louder* dedication and determination, we can succeed. Think about these actions and suggestions concerning setting goals for improved health:

Setting Goals

- Share your goals with a close friend or relative.
- If you're a believer, ask God to help you set your goals.
- Make both short-term and long-term goals.
- Make your goals reasonable and believable.
- Make your health goals a high priority in your life.
- Put your goals in writing and post them someplace highly visible. If they're easy to see, they'll be easy to keep in mind.
- You don't have to have deadlines for your goals as long as you're making progress.
- Ask God to help you "make it happen."

Call your mother frequently and spend time with people you love. Focus on your priorities.

CULTIVATE CHARACTER

Life Is a Journey

We should try to make the most of what we are given.

We are all on a journey called life. This was brought to our attention at a recent memorial service for a man who traveled a very interesting, productive and rewarding journey in his full life. Family members spoke about those who were part of his journey and the love and respect that was shared by this man and for him.

It was a wonderful service. You could easily tell that most who attended were emotionally moved. It was both sad and joyful, as are most memorial services. It inspired me to think about what more I should be doing now and in the future for my family, my friends, my associates and my community.

If there are things that could and should be done, perhaps now is the time to make some of these things come to life—time to make new things happen on our journey.

Included in the program for the memorial service were Stephan Grellet's words:

I expect to pass through this world but once;
any good thing therefore that I can do, or any
kindness that I can show to any fellow creature,
let me do it now; let me not defer or
neglect it, for I shall not pass this way again.

Knowing that life is a journey makes it possible to believe there are choices and different paths available to us. We don't have to keep going in the same direction, at the same speed, taking all the same turns day in and out. We can do as Stephan Grellet tells us by doing any good thing or showing any kindness to a fellow creature on our new journey. We will at some time not pass this way again.

Yogi Berra said, "When you come to a fork in the road, take it." This is one of Yogi's most often quoted sayings because it is so humorous. It is that indeed. But it also has a good message when looking at life's journey. That's because it's very easy and comfortable when you come to a fork in life's road just to stop and wait for the fork to go away. This may, however, be an opportunity to help someone else to take the right road and share the journey with him. Making this kind of decision might involve taking risks, but with them might very well be great rewards.

Robert Frost's "The Road Not Taken" has so much significance about life's journey. As a reminder, the first and last verses are included:

> *Two roads diverged in a yellow wood,*
> *And sorry I could not travel both*
> *And be one traveler, long I stood*
> *To where it bent in the undergrowth;*
>
> *I shall be telling this with a sigh*
> *Somewhere ages and ages hence;*
> *Two roads diverged in a wood, and I—*
> *I took the one less traveled by,*
> *And that has made all the difference.*

Because we will not pass this way again and life's journey is full of such wonderful opportunities for doing good things and doing acts of kindness, this might be the right time to set some life journey goals. Set many life journey goals, because even if we don't reach all of them, we undoubtedly will go higher than we would have if we hadn't set goals at all.

Setting goals, sharing a fork in the road, traveling a road less traveled by with acts of kindness, and doing good things will help to make the journey more successful and rewarding.

Set goals for a new journey.

CARING

Saying Thank You

These two small words can mean a great deal to others.

In the United States we have our own Thanksgiving holiday. It is a wonderful day when we are reminded to give thanks for our many blessings. It is our country's holiday, and we should give thanks that we are fortunate enough to live in this great country. This is the favorite holiday of the year for many people and families.

This time of year, we should remember not only to give thanks to God for all He has done for us, but also to others who deserve our gratitude.

As an example of this, I want to share a little story. When William Stidger taught at a well-known university, he once reflected upon the great number of un-thanked people in his life, those who helped nurture him, inspire him, or who cared enough to leave a lasting impression on him. One was a schoolteacher he'd not heard of in many years, but he remembered that she'd gone out of her way to instill in him a love of verse.

As a result, Stidger had loved poetry all his life. So he wrote her a letter of thanks. The reply he received, written in the feeble scrawl of the aged, began, "My Dear Willie." He was delighted. He was now over 50, bald, and a professor. He didn't think there was a person left on the planet who would call him "Willie."

Here's the letter: "My Dear Willie, I cannot tell you how much your note meant to me. I'm in my eighties, living alone in a small room, cooking my own meals, lonely, and like the last leaf of autumn, lingering behind. You will be interested to know that I taught school for 50 years, and yours is the first note of appreciation I ever received. It came on a blue-cold morning and cheered me as nothing has in many years." Not prone to cry easily, Stidger wept over that note.

She was one of the great un-thanked people from his past. You know them—we all do. Mother Teresa said, "Kind words can be short and easy to speak, but their echoes are truly endless."

How many people are there who have had a significant influence in our lives who are un-thanked, not just by us, but by all those with whom they share every day. There are many teachers such as Professor Stidger's English teacher. There are probably others you can think of, such as a favorite Sunday School teacher, a coach, a music teacher, a relative, a friend, a fraternity or sorority member or who all else? Why not take the time to send them a kind letter or give them a call?

A good friend of mine for more than 30 years retired from ABB. At a retirement celebration for him, I was reminded of all the good things he had done for our company, for the customers and employees. How do you adequately thank someone like that for his friendship and his many contributions? Is it enough to just say I feel blessed to have had you as a friend and business associate for so many years, and thanks for all you have done? Probably not, but it's better than not saying anything at all!

Think of some un-thanked persons and thank them. Do it again and again.

9

COMMUNICATING

Keep in Touch

Christmas cards once a year are not enough.

Dr. Thomas H. Troeger, the J. Edward and Ruth Cox Lantz Professor of Christian Communication at Yale Divinity School, was a guest speaker at the 2009 Stratten Series at the First Christian Church in Wichita Falls, Texas. Dr. Troeger is a gifted speaker, teacher, writer, preacher, flutist, poet and a very good cross-country and downhill skier.

During one of his sermons, titled "Love So Ancient and So New," he told about a gift he was given when he graduated from the Virginia Theological Seminary a number of years ago. The gift was a replica of the famous painting by Michelangelo, *The Creation of Adam,* on the ceiling of the Sistine Chapel. Completed in 1511, this painting illustrates the Biblical story from the Book of Genesis, in which God the Father breathes life into Adam, the first man. It shows God with his hand and finger reaching out to Adam's hand and extended finger—almost touching. You probably can remember and visualize this well-known painting.

Dr. Troeger said the painting looked much like the original, except that his had a bubble with words coming out of God's mouth. God was saying to Adam, "Keep in touch." Thomas Troeger keeps this painting in his office as a constant reminder of the importance of keeping in touch with God. He told stories about how often this helped him personally, as well as with those whom he was counseling. His sermon was about keeping in touch with God with the heart, not just at a distance with only the fingers almost touching.

Keeping in touch with family and friends is also very important. Perhaps, many of us could use our own special painting in our office or our home to remind us that keeping in touch should be a top priority in life. The visual reminder doesn't have to be a Michelangelo painting. It could be a family picture, a painting of a favorite vacation spot, or anything that will work for you. The painting or picture is probably already in your home or office. All that is needed is to make an association of the picture with the value of keeping in touch the right way.

I think we all like the idea of keeping in touch—not just saying it, but doing it. Many people include "Let's keep in touch" as a regular part of saying good-bye, and quite often without much meaning. This could be considered almost finger-touching as in Michelangelo's painting. What we should be looking for is more than that. Keeping in touch from the heart is what we really want.

Keeping in touch can mean a lot of different things. It could mean just sending Christmas cards once a year or it could mean much more. I remember some good friends in Boston saying their good-byes to us when we moved to York, Pennsylvania. After saying, "Let's keep in touch," my friend paused and then added, "Have a good life." It was a very meaningful thing to say. He was being realistic about the future. We would be keeping in touch remotely with Christmas cards, and that would be about it ... and it was okay.

With family and good friends, keeping in touch with only cards is not okay. John Burroughs said, "I still find each day too short for all the thoughts I want to think, all the walks I want to take, all the books I want to read and all the friends I want to see."

Well, John, I believe the answer is to focus on the priorities that are the most important. I would recommend keeping in touch with the friends whom you want to see at the top of your list.

Make keeping in touch with family and friends a top priority.

CULTIVATE CHARACTER

Have a Wise Companion

Common sense is a true and trusted friend.

Let's wish in the New Year with a very good companion: Common Sense. At this time of year, it is especially important to consider what we want to accomplish during the next year. This could also mean thinking about the help that might be needed to be successful in reaching our goals.

This fine old character, common sense, could very well be the help we have been wanting. And you know it is right out there in our own back yard waiting to join with us to do good things. All we have to do is invite common sense to be a part of our team and then to use and listen to him or her often.

Who is this possible common sense companion and how would you describe him? Well, John Billings described him: "Common sense is the knack of seeing things as they are, and doing things as they ought to be done."

What does common sense bring to the party? There are many ways that common sense's personality and talents could be described. One way is to say that common sense tells us to pay attention to the obvious. Listening to our companion, common sense, is not always as easy as it sounds. That's because we all have vivid imaginations and we tend to get lost in fantasies ... sometimes with unrealistic possibilities.

I heard the story of common sense talking to a third-year medical student during morning rounds. They examined a patient with a black tongue. The intern assigned to that patient had researched all the causes of a black tongue and was eager to demonstrate his new knowledge. As the intern started to lecture the students, the attending physician interrupted him and asked the patient if he used black cough drops. The patient smiled, opened the drawer of his night table, and took out a package of Smith Brothers black cough drops.

The intern was embarrassed, because he was so focused on being a doctor that he forgot to ask his patient an obvious question. He needed a companion like common sense to be with him that day. The doctor who told this story says he still has a vivid memory of that intern and that lesson: Use common sense and pay attention to the obvious.

How valuable is having common sense as a companion and a part of your personal team? I think its value and importance to success were expressed by Thomas Edison: "The three great essentials to achieve anything worthwhile are first, hard work; second, stick-to-itiveness; third, common sense." We can't go into Thomas Edison's mind or know what he was thinking, but I'll bet many of his inventions came about by using common sense.

Consider these two equations:

$$KNOWLEDGE + COMMON\ SENSE = WISDOM$$
$$KNOWLEDGE - COMMON\ SENSE = NONSENSE$$

How important is common sense? If it weren't for common sense, it's hard to tell where our country would be today. In January of 1776, Thomas Paine anonymously wrote *Common Sense*. This was an instant best-seller, both in the colonies and in Europe. Because of it, Paine became internationally famous.

Paine's political pamphlet brought the rising revolutionary sentiment into sharp focus by placing blame for the suffering of the colonies directly on the reigning British monarch, George III.

First and foremost, *Common Sense* advocated an immediate declaration of independence. Not long after publication, the spirit of Paine's argument found resonance in the American Declaration of Independence.

Written at the outset of the Revolution, *Common Sense* became the motivator of the times. It encouraged the colonists to strengthen their resolve, resulting in our independence.

Maybe our political leaders today should go back and read Thomas Paine's *Common Sense* and try to incorporate common sense into their leadership styles. They should use the equation "knowledge + common sense = wisdom" more and the equation "knowledge − common sense = nonsense" less. And they should listen to John Billings: "Common sense is the knack of seeing things as they are, and doing things as they ought to be done."

Plan to have common sense as a companion this year.

COACHING

Enhance Your Sense of Humor

Sense of humor is common sense dancing.

One way to turn up the volume in *Actions Speak Louder* is to have a wise companion in the future. This wise companion, introduced in a previous action, is common sense. We are reminded by Thomas Edison of the value of having this companion: "The three great essentials to achieve anything worthwhile are first, hard work; second, stick-to-itiveness; third, common sense." Common sense quite often has a very good and close friend named Sense of Humor.

William James, an American philosopher and psychologist, said, "Common sense and a sense of humor are the same things, moving at different speeds. A sense of humor is just common sense dancing." Thinking about common sense dancing has to bring a smile to your face and it probably makes you want to share this thought in some way with others. A sense of humor is to be shared, you know, although it is quite alright to enjoy your own sense of humor when you are alone.

What is a sense of humor, or better yet, what is a **good** sense of humor? We know the benefits of laughter and the pleasure it brings to so many people every day. Research finds that life is healthier with humor, which can help us cope better with pain, strengthen our immune system, reduce stress and even help us live longer. No matter our age, wealth, race, or living situation, life is good when laughter is frequent. So knowing all this, what can we do to enhance our sense of humor?

Mark Twain once said, "Studying humor is like dissecting a frog—you may know a lot, but you end up with a dead frog." Mark Twain definitely had a very good sense of humor. Can't you just picture him quietly sitting by himself writing the many witty sayings he left for us to enjoy? He must have had a continual feeling of joy and satisfaction, and of course, a smile on his face. We can learn from him and others as we try to grow our own sense of humor.

Tips to Enhance Your Sense of Humor

- If something doesn't go the way you expected or planned, think of the situation as being amusing. This is especially effective when traveling, because if a plane is delayed, your baggage is lost, or a hotel has given away your room reservation, it doesn't do any good to get mad. It is much better to find a way to laugh at the problem than to get upset and stressed. It also makes people much more willing to help you find a solution if you have a sense of humor.

- Smile often. A smile and a laugh aren't the same, but they do live in the same neighborhood. It is good to smile at all the simple pleasures that occur every day. Think about counting the number of times you smile each day. If your day's total isn't at least twenty, then it might be worthwhile to explore whether you are depressed or overly stressed.

- At family dinners or with gatherings of friends, ask others to share something that recently happened to them or something that was funny or embarrassing. Be prepared to share some personal experience that you found to be funny. Also tell how you turned a bad situation into an amusing one, and how it worked to your advantage. This can happen often if you just let it happen.

- Search the Internet for funny stories or jokes that you can share with others. If you are one of those people who can't seem to remember jokes, write them down in a little notebook and review them before getting together with friends or family. Our regular Thursday lunch group has a member who brings e-mails and entertains us with his readings. A group of 8 to 12 men laughing is perhaps disturbing to others in the restaurant, but we find them leaning over to listen to the reading. One man at a nearby table even fell out of his chair trying to hear. And you know, he laughed about it and so did we.

- Some say an apple a day keeps the doctor away. Others say a laugh a day keeps the doctor away. I say eat an apple a day and laugh more than once a day—just don't do them at the same time.

There are many ways to enjoy and enhance your sense of humor. I'll bet you have many ideas for making this happen. One way is to spend time with happy people.

Count the number of times you smiled today. Make it more tomorrow!

Focus on Using Proper Grammar

Using the correct words gives a favorable impression.

Who or whom knows when to use good or well and if it's or its time to give advise or advice?

It seems that the incorrect use of most of these words shows up in writing rather than the spoken word. This can give the reader an unfavorable impression, especially when the wrong words are used in résumés or important letters. Proper grammar can be very important. It can mean the difference between getting a job interview and having your résumé thrown into a waste paper basket, never to be seen again.

Last week, I was visiting with an old friend at our church library. She mentioned that she enjoyed reading the articles each week and especially the ones about grammar and manners. She suggested that I do another one on grammar and include examples about lie and lay.

She shared with me a recent experience she had had with a local doctor, who told her to lay down on the bed in her hospital room. Being an English teacher for many years, she felt obligated to correct this foreign-born doctor. She said it should be "lie" down on the bed. He told her that he thought "lie" was correct, but the nurses in the hospital had told him it should be "lay" down. The next time he saw her, he told her to lie down. She was pleased, but the nurses probably were not.

I have been surprised, but pleasantly so, that grammar articles have generated such a high level of interest in our community. Since I am not an English teacher, I don't feel qualified to go into much depth about really technical issues in sentence structure and diagramming, but I do appreciate good grammar.

I very much dislike hearing or seeing bad grammar in business, because it is a reflection on the professionalism of the company. One time, we even hired a local college professor of English to teach a grammar class at ABB. It was fun and successful. Attending the grammar class was not optional.

So (it's or its) time to have a few more examples and see if this will be (good or well) (advise or advice) for the readers of this book and (their, there or they're) friends and business associates.

First, let's look at my friend's example of lie or lay. There is confusion here, and it is understandable, because lay is the past tense of lie as well as being the present tense of itself. Remember it is lie/lay/lain and it is lay/laid/laid. Okay, this is somewhat technical and we learned this all years ago. How do we remember what to say or write?

- Lie—to be in a horizontal position
- Lay—put something in position

Next example is using good or well. I was just reminded of this after I gave a short talk at the Rotary Club, and a friend reminded me that I had used good when I should have used well, or well when it should have been good. Either way, it was well of him to point this out to me or was it good of him to point this out? I vote for "good." The question really is, was it "nice" of him to point this out?

Good is an adjective and well is normally an adverb. Good describes nouns or pronouns, and well describes verbs and sometimes adjectives. Some examples:

The coffee tasted (well or good) this morning. It better taste good.

The pitcher is looking (good or well) today. Depends on whether you are referring to his pitching, or if you are saying he has been sick and is now looking better.

I do not feel very (good or well). As an adjective, "well" means healthy. So here it is "well."

It's and its are two little words that are often used incorrectly. This probably happens due to carelessness rather than not knowing which is right. "Its" is possessive, and "it's" is a contraction of "it is."

I think the same is true about using advice and advise. You advise and you ask for advice because "advice" is the noun and "advise" is a verb.

Who or whom? It's really not very important in speaking because "whom" in casual conversation is generally being phased out, but not in formal, written documents. In the first sentence of this article, it would be "who" knows when to use ... and it would be to "whom" would I give the right answer. If the answer to the question is he or she, use "who," and if the answer is her or him, use "whom."

Have fun with good grammar.

Read a book from the past that made an impression on you, such as *To Kill a Mockingbird.*

COMMITTING

Get Motivated

Motivation is the key to success.

Goals for this year: plans, resolutions, commitments and schedules. Many of us have been spending time these past few weeks thinking about what we are going to do this year. What do we plan to accomplish? How important is it that we succeed in what we are planning or the goals that we have set? Are we really serious about making these things happen? Or probably most important of all, are we motivated enough to get started and to continue throughout the year?

These are good questions. Just the other day, I was told that a friend of mine had stopped smoking January 1 and hadn't had a cigarette so far this year. It is a good start. It's not the first time he has tried to stop smoking, but I hope this will be the one that counts. For most of us who have successfully quit smoking, we practiced quitting many times before we got it right. I congratulated him on his accomplishment, because receiving recognition for such a challenge can help to reinforce his determination.

He told me that he was really motivated this time because of health issues. Knowing you have a health problem that can be avoided by stopping smoking should be a huge motivator. When I stopped smoking about 35 years ago, I was motivated because I didn't want to get to the point that it would be too late to avoid health problems. I convinced myself that I really wasn't giving up something when I quit ... I was gaining many things that more than offset the little pleasure that I got from smoking. It worked for me, and I'm quite sure my friend's motivation will work for him as well.

Last fall, I was talking to a local doctor about his methods and programs for his patients who want to lose weight. He said there are many good programs that work if the patient sticks to the plan. The lack of success for many is not because of the program chosen. The problem is the patient. The patient is simply not motivated enough to be serious about losing weight. He said they all say they want to lose weight, but are sometimes unwilling to make long-term life style changes. They don't want to accept the fact that to lose weight, you must eat less and exercise more. There's no magic about it ... there is just the need for motivation.

Motivation shouldn't be a fleeting kind of thing. Zig Ziglar said, "People often say that motivation doesn't last. Well, neither does bathing—that's why we recommend it daily."

Ten Tips to Help Motivation Last

1. Have a single most important goal that is the top priority of all your plans.
2. Be enthused and excited about your goal. Try to make it a fun thing—not something you dread.
3. Stick with it. Don't cheat, because the only one you would be cheating is you—nobody else.
4. Build on your success. Start small and celebrate and enjoy your success each week.
5. Stay focused. Think about your goal daily and commit to doing the right things each day.
6. Avoid problem situations in which the temptation to cheat might be difficult to handle.
7. Post your goal in very visible locations, including home, office and your car.
8. Daily, think about all the benefits, not the difficulties. Know that you are the one winning in a big way by reaching your goal.
9. Get support. It is hard to accomplish something alone.
10. Eliminate negative thoughts. Replace them with positive thoughts.

Motivation takes energy and focus. Having a worthwhile goal is important enough to commit the focus and energy necessary for success. That is the motivation which will lead to success.

Select which of the ten tips will be most important for your success.

COMMUNICATING

Focus on Communication

Both verbal and written conversations frequently are misunderstood.

I am continually amazed at how often even simple communications are misunderstood. It happens every day with both verbal and written communications. You know that for someone to recognize the message was misunderstood means the miscommunication was caught or detected by one or both parties. Otherwise, you would be getting the wrong message without knowing it. This being the case, just think how often we receive the wrong message and maybe never know what the right message or communication was supposed to be. What have we missed or what are we missing today?

Don't you think better communication and perhaps not missing the message that was intended would add to your happiness and the happiness of those with whom you communicate? If I am communicating correctly, the answer to this question should be yes.

Let's think about ways to focus on better communication. The following is a list of questions that you might want to consider when preparing for either written or verbal communication. You won't have time to review this list in normal daily communication, but the basics could be with you and should be considered.

Ask yourself these questions about your communication

- Why am I doing this?
- What do I want to accomplish?
- Who needs to be involved and who needs to know?
- Is it clear who should be doing what and when? Who has the ball?
- Are the time frame and expectations clear and reasonable?
- Do I have all the information necessary to communicate properly?
- Are my attitude and frame of mind right for this communication now?

- Should I take additional time to think and review this communication?
- Can I shorten the communication? Can I make it clearer?
- What should be **highlighted** or emphasized?
- Is there anyone who could be hurt, offended, disappointed or mad when they receive this communication? If so, consider making changes.
- Solicit feedback and ask questions so you can be sure your communication was understood.

Much of this also applies to e-mail communication. Communications by e-mail are so easy and so fast and generally require little time or little thought. And, this is the problem—too easy, too fast and too little thought given to the content.

A few suggestions about e-mail communication

- Reread the e-mail communication before sending it.
- Use Spell Check.
- Make the e-mail as short as possible.
- Since it is so easy to send copies, make sure it is clear who is to do what.
- Do not use e-mail to be critical, to send bad news, to communicate controversial issues. Do all of these things face to face or at least verbally.
- If you are responding to an e-mail that made you mad, wait at least a day before responding.
- When replying, make sure those receiving copies are the ones you want to receive your e-mail.
- Check to make sure your attachments are correct.
- Recognize that your e-mail, with your name on it, could be shared with any number of people.
- Make sure you have the right e-mail address. You don't want to send the e-mail to the wrong person. This happens.

Remember that once something is written and sent, or something is said, you cannot get it back. Consider not putting an address on your e-mail until you are absolutely sure you want to send it. That way it won't be sent inadvertently.

Commit to becoming a better communicator with family, friends and associates.

COACHING

Advice for the Graduate

Dedication and determination are important for any goal in life.

There is a time of year when seniors in high school and college are experiencing new feelings and emotions. They probably are mostly good feelings. It is only natural, however, for the good emotions to be mixed with anxiety, some nervousness and questions about what happens next. Whether you're graduating from high school or college, you'll be moving into a new phase of your life, and this means different opportunities and challenges for you.

What will the new phase be like? How can I make the most of this time in my life? What should I be doing? These are good questions. You probably have been given lots of answers to them and have received advice ranging from your commencement speaker's message to thoughts from your family, friends, teachers and others.

I would like to suggest that you keep in mind two crucial characteristics of success. They are dedication and determination. These two are very important no matter what your goals or plans for the next phase in your life. Think about these as you read through the following suggestions:

Advice for the Graduating Senior

- Many suggest that you select a field of study or a job for which you have a strong passion. This makes good sense. Try to make it happen.
- Work hard, but also have fun. Work hard first before you have your share of fun. Balance is important.
- Use your time wisely. Don't waste it on foolish things.
- Do the right things. You know what that means. Use common sense.
- Call your mom frequently, and not just to ask for money.
- Get involved—volunteer for extra work or committees. Don't forget your church or the community.

- Plan to assume leadership positions. Go for being president of the organization or head of the committee. Later on, you will see that most people remember who the president was—not the vice president.
- Spend time with winners. Choose your friends and associates wisely. It's true that birds of a feather flock together.
- Don't get lazy if you have extra spare time.
- Don't let your faith go on vacation.
- Pick your boss or your professors wisely if you can. Do research on them.
- Get to know your professors or other business associates outside your department.
- It is true that "what goes around, comes around." This means to never burn bridges.
- If you are having problems with a class or a job assignment, discuss it with your professor or with your boss. They want you to succeed.
- Study and read more than what is expected. Do more than the minimum to just get by. If you are asked for bread, give them cake.
- Remember moderation.
- Spend time with people you love.

Benjamin Franklin said, "Early to bed and early to rise makes a man healthy, wealthy and wise." It's easy to remember these words, but it's not the real world for graduating seniors. And a friend of Franklin's added, "Early to bed and early to rise and your girl goes out with other guys."

How about modifying Franklin's advice for graduates?

- To bed—not too late
- To rise—early enough to follow Lombardi time (show up 15 minutes early for scheduled meetings or classes)
- To participate—enough energy to do your best
- To learn—alert enough to catch and understand everything
- To commit—don't miss any classes or business meetings

I think Benjamin Franklin would say that if you do these "To's," you will be healthy, wealthy and wise and your girl won't go out with other guys.

To follow much of the advice listed here will require dedication and determination on your part. It will be worth it!

Enjoy time together now with the classmates you won't be with next year.

COMMITTING

Another Phase of Life

The graduate's transition to college can be difficult for some parents.

A previous *Actions Speak Louder* action provided advice for the graduating senior. A number of suggestions were listed:

- Call your mom frequently.
- Work hard, but also have fun.
- Use your time wisely.
- Do the right things.
- Spend time with winners.

There were a number of other suggestions as well, because the senior is moving into another phase of his or her life. Life is made up of different phases that are all good and which offer wonderful opportunities, as well as significant challenges. High school was one phase; college is another.

There are also phases for parents of a graduating senior. Moving from one phase to another can be emotional for parents. The high-school phase is one in which parents are generally very involved. A great deal of time is spent attending games, events, concerts and plays. It is a phase in which many parents are able to relive their own high-school experiences through their kids. This can be either good or bad for both the parents and the student. Obviously, the goal is to make it positive.

The next phase will be different, and this leaves a definite void in the parents' time and thoughts. It can be sad to think that you won't be going to watch your son play football anymore, or to watch your daughter march in the high-school band, or whatever you have enjoyed so much these past few years.

Here are a few suggestions to fill this void and make the transition from the high-school phase to the college phase positive:

Advice for the Parents of a Graduating Senior

- Celebrate the graduation and the successes your senior achieved.
- Write a letter to your senior saying how proud you are of him or her. List his or her most memorable events or accomplishments. This will make a nice record for all of you in the future.
- Be positive about the future and don't dwell on the past. Remember it, appreciate it, but don't continue to relive it—time to move on.
- Plan to replace the time spent at these past high-school events with things you have wanted to do. It is important to have things that you can look forward to on a regular basis. Some examples could be spending more time with your spouse, or playing more tennis or golf, or committing to getting back in shape. How about writing a book or a series of short stories?
- Recognize that your feeling of giving up something very special to you is normal. It is also healthy to let go when the time is right—and the time is right with this new phase.
- Be happy for your senior. Remember how you felt when you moved into this new phase. You didn't think you were giving something up; you were excited about it.
- Keep in touch with your son or daughter, but not too much. Keep the communication open.
- Your advice is important, but remember, a good coach doesn't teach basics during an important game. You have already coached and have given a good background of basics; now it is time for your graduate to grow and apply these fundamentals.
- Appreciate the feelings that your spouse might have. They might be different from yours, but together you can make the most of the new phase.
- Do what you can to make visits home fun and positive. Make it so that your son or daughter looks forward to coming back to be with you and friends, rather than a time for getting griped at because of late hours or whatever.
- Plan to enjoy this phase and get the most out of it that you can.

Write a letter to your graduate telling him or her how proud you are of all they have done in high school.

COMMITTING

Just Do It

Don't hesitate if you think it's the right thing to do.

Some years ago, an acquaintance of ours died quite suddenly. Although we knew the couple reasonably well, we did not consider ourselves close friends. So, we discussed whether or not we should visit the widow at her home. We debated whether this would be the right thing to do, or if we would seem to be imposing on her during a difficult time.

We did visit her that evening, and it was absolutely the right thing to have done. She was gracious and very much appreciated our caring about her.

Right then, we decided that if there were a question of doing something, or not, in the future, we would ...

Just do it!

It has proven to be the right philosophy 100% of the time. So now, when there is a question about whether or not to do something, we just do it. I think that if you are considering doing something, you are considering it for good reasons, and probably deep down inside, you know the right answer. We have found it is easier to just do it than to try and second-guess ourselves.

Another very important consideration is whether, in the future, we would regret not doing something. If an opportunity to do something is presented to you, how will you feel a few years from now if you choose not to do it? It is not likely that you will have this particular opportunity again. This reminds me of a well-known, but seldom used saying:

If not now, when?

In these days, when so many things are just pushed off and procrastination seems to be so commonplace, this saying—"If not now, when?"—isn't heard very often. Maybe it isn't even understood very well, or at least not openly acknowledged by some. But we know what it means, don't we?

I think this also has to do with being willing to take some risks in life. It sometimes appears that successful people are lucky. Some may think it is just a matter of being in the right place at the right time. Maybe these lucky ones were the kind of people who believed in just doing it. Maybe they also recognized opportunities, were prepared to take some risks and felt, "If not now, when?" Or perhaps they knew and understood the following saying:

If it is to be, it is up to me.

Today is a good time to reflect on what is going on right now. Are there opportunities out there that should be considered? Are there projects that should be started? Is there a part in a play that you might like to have? Is there an athletic team that you would like to try out for? Is there another job that you would rather be doing? Is there a friend you should be spending more time with? Is there a family member who needs some special attention? With any of these kinds of opportunities, it is good to think about these same thoughts:

If it is to be, it is up to me.

If not now, when?

Just do it!

Alfred Lord Tennyson wrote, "Tis better to have loved and lost than never to have loved at all." I believe all this goes together with a kind of harmony that leads to happiness and success. Why put yourself in a position in which you might have regrets later because you didn't "Just do it"? Or you waited for someone else to do it and forgot about "If it is to be, it is up to me." Or you delayed and forgot about "If not now, when?"

Go for it. You know it really is up to you.

Think of at least one thing that has been delayed, which you will pursue, and "just do it."

COACHING

Listen to Charles Dickens

Listen carefully when considering significant changes.

If you are considering making a job change, or any other significant change in your life, listen to what Charles Dickens had to say in *A Tale of Two Cities:*

> *It was the best of times, it was the worst of times. It was the age of wisdom, it was the age of foolishness, it was the epoch of belief, it was the epoch of incredulity, it was the season of Light, it was the season of Darkness, it was the spring of hope, it was the winter of despair, we had everything before us, we had nothing before us, we were all going direct to Heaven, we were all going direct the other way.*

What does this mean as it relates to considering making a job change or any other major change in one's life? Let's focus on making a job change in this *Actions Speak Louder* action. The thought process, however, would be similar for making other kinds of decisions.

"It was the best of times"—Evaluate your present or most recent job. Think about the past, the present and your vision of the future. What parts of the job do you enjoy most? When do you feel really good about your contributions and your value to the organization? Consider all the positives, including relationships, about your present situation. If you change jobs, you will be giving these up. You know you give up the good as well as the bad when you leave.

"It was the worst of times"—What do you really dislike about your present job or situation? Is this something new, or has this unhappiness existed for some time? Is it the job, or is the problem related to those with whom you work? Is this unpleasant situation or job assignment likely to change? Is there anything you can personally do to improve what is bothering you? If you change jobs, will you be able to improve this situation, or will it be going with you? Some jobs, for some people, are just plain unpleasant. It doesn't make sense to change one unpleasant situation for another unpleasant one.

"It was the age of wisdom"—Be wise in analyzing your situation. Be honest with yourself and be willing to accept the fact that some of the unhappiness might be something you created. Perhaps being wise is just recognizing there are better opportunities available if you take the responsibility for making some positive changes.

"It was the age of foolishness"—When considering changing jobs, don't do anything foolish. Be sure you don't burn any bridges. Be diligent and thorough in analyzing the new job, the benefits, the pay structure, the job description, expectations and timing. Don't make a change without having a "for sure" job waiting for you. Take the time to make sure all the paperwork is complete, you passed the physical and there are no open issues.

"It was the epoch of belief"—Are your expectations for the new job, the new company, realistic, and do you fully understand and believe what is expected of you? Do you believe what they are telling you directly or indirectly? Do you have to reach certain levels of performance before you obtain the position or income level that you desire? Is all of this in writing and is it clear? Clear up all assumptions and have all the answers you need before making a change. Neither you nor the new company wants to have any misunderstandings.

"It was the epoch of incredulity"—Yes, it is the right time not to believe blindly what you want to hear or want to have happen. It is the time to question; it is the time to seek clarity and understanding. The goal is to turn incredulity to belief through facts, documentation and confirmation.

"It was the season of Light"—What are the very best things that can happen with the new job or position? Are these things, whatever they are, possible, and can you make them happen? Is attaining these objectives worth making a change?

"It was the season of Darkness"—Likewise, consider the worst things that could happen if you change jobs. How really bad could it be and how easily and quickly could you recover? It is a good idea to consider the best and the worst scenarios that could happen with the change. The actual situation will be somewhere between the best and the worst—probably closer to the best.

The rest of the paragraph from *A Tale of Two Cities* fits into the above considerations. Mainly, the recommendation is to think seriously about this famous and often quoted selection, as it has to do with honestly and objectively analyzing your present situation and future opportunities before making a change.

When considering making a job change, don't let your performance level drop off.

19

CARING

Make Someone Happy

It's a wonderful opportunity for all of us.

What could possibly be more important today than doing something to make someone happy? Especially someone you really care about. Read these words and imagine that Jimmy Durante is singing this song just for you:

Make someone happy,
Make just one someone happy;
Make just one heart the heart you sing to.
One smile that cheers you,
One face that lights when it nears you,
One girl you're everything to.

Fame if you win it,
Comes and goes in a minute.
Where's the real stuff in life to cling to?
Love is the answer,
Someone to love is the answer.
Once you've found her, build your world around her.

Make someone happy,
Make just one someone happy,
And you will be happy too.

We all want to make someone happy, and that brings happiness to us. The problem is, we forget or we get too involved with our own busy schedule, and before we know it months have gone by. That's why we need a gentle reminder every now and then. Maybe this song and action can be that reminder for at least the next few days/weeks/months. It's up to you to decide for how long and to invent your own reminder if different from this song.

"I did it my way" is the theme and the message in another *Actions Speak Louder* action and came originally from a newspaper article. The day that article ran in our local paper, a friend of ours pulled over in front of us as we were walking early in the morning around Midwestern State University. She rolled down her window and starting singing, "I Did it My Way." It was so neat to hear her sing this song, which she did with a lot of feeling. Pretty voice too. She made my day.

Maybe you'll want to sing "Make Someone Happy." The messages in this song are good: "love is the answer"; "one heart the heart you sing to"; "make just someone happy and you will be happy too."

How do you make someone happy? It is a personal thing, but here are a few suggestions:

- Compliment someone in an honest and sincere way.
- Praise someone for something they have done. Do this with the person's boss or good friend.
- Plan to do something your special person would like to do that you would normally not choose.
- Tell them you were thinking of them when something important happened, or that a very good movie or book made you think of them.
- Help them with something they are working on, or just help with the daily chores.
- Be a real gentleman—open the car door for her, as an example.
- Of course, remember birthdays and anniversaries. What other special times could you remember that might be especially meaningful?
- Help someone to think big. Encourage someone by saying, "you should do that" or "you should write a book."
- Share good experiences with others by making recommendations of things you like.
- Tell someone you love him or her.
- Think of something that this person really doesn't like to do, then do it.
- Share a funny story or joke.

I'm sure you have many other actions that you use or can think of using to make someone happy. Most of us just need to do it more often. Maybe this could be some sort of resolution beginning today.

 Commit to "make someone happy" more often.

20

COMMITTING

Y Not Make a Difference?

U can do it.

I read an article recently about an individual who was determined to make a difference in someone's life each day of the week that ended in a "Y." I had to think about this for a few minutes, but, yes, I did figure out that he meant every day. All of us are making a difference in this life, but are we making the right differences as often as we want? Should it be every day?

Consider starting every morning asking yourself, "What one thing could I do today that would make a positive difference in my life and the lives of those around me?" Know that you do not have to do something earth shattering to make a difference. It's often the little things that have the greatest impact.

Some examples of these little things could include the following: some little act of kindness, a warm greeting, a smile that brightens a bad day, personal recognition, words of encouragement, a sincere compliment, a friendly word, a helping hand or a sympathetic ear. These are the things that can be done every day without any financial cost or personal sacrifice. There are many, many more little things and acts that can just happen if we are on the lookout for them.

When you make a difference with just one person, you have no way of knowing how far-reaching your action will be and for how long the effects of what you have done will be felt. The result of making a difference in someone's life oftentimes has a multiplying effect. It can be contagious in a good way—something you want to catch and pass on. It's all healthy. Think about this: "If everyone lit just one little candle, what a bright world this would be." What a bright world this would be with many thousands of people making a difference daily.

Thoughts on Making a Difference

- Volunteer where your talents, interests and prayers lead you.

- Look for opportunities to make a difference.
- Be aware of those who might be hurting or in need of help.
- Be kind and thoughtful—be yourself.
- Where can you make a difference with family members and friends?
- When you see an area of need, don't just assume someone else is taking care of it.
- Visit people who are homebound or in nursing homes.
- If there is a question of whether or not to do something, just do it.
- If someone is looking for bread, give them cake.
- Set an example by going the extra mile.
- Contact your university or a local university to see if there are students with special needs for whom help might make the difference in their staying in school or dropping out for financial reasons.
- Consider providing help for families whose father or mother is in the service and away in Iraq or Afghanistan. Maybe it's baby-sitting or providing some meals or even financial assistance.
- Talk to your church or your minister about how you can make a difference. Why not start making a difference each day that ends with a "y"?

 Make a difference in someone's life today.

21

COUNTRY

What Happened to Telling the Truth?

Some always seem to get a pass.

When you go to your doctor, you expect him, to the best of his ability, to tell you the truth. There is no reason to doubt him unless there is a very unusual situation. The same is true with your lawyer and your accountant. Why would they not tell you the truth?

Of course, your minister is as honest as the day is long, and you would expect nothing but the truth from him. Teachers are known for truthfulness, because the kinds of people who choose education as their profession are good, honest, caring people.

The question today is, why can't we trust our politicians? They don't seem to think they have to tell the truth. It is okay to say anything they feel will help them get elected. This is the case both individually and as a group. If this isn't the truth, how is it possible for each politician to take a vow to uphold the constitution and to represent the people, when all senators and representatives in one party vote one way, and all in the other party vote the other way? Don't they have a conscience?

The approval rating of Congress is at an all-time low. It is not surprising, because they are not representing the people and they cannot be trusted.

What I believe we all have to do is think about what our candidates are saying and decide whether these are just words or real commitments, and if they mean what they are saying. I would look out for words such as *never, always, promise, pledge,* and similar words.

When a politician uses the word *never,* it makes me think of *HMS Pinafore* by Gilbert and Sullivan. Just picture these words and substitute the politician's name or position in the appropriate places.

Captain: *I am the Captain of the Pinafore.*

Chorus:	*And a right good captain, too!*
Captain:	*You're very, very good,* *And be it understood,* *I command a right good crew.*
Chorus:	*We're very, very good,* *And be it understood,* *He commands a right good crew.*
Captain:	*Though related to a peer,* *I can hand, reef, and steer,* *And ship a selvage;* *I am never known to quail* *At the fury of a gale,* *And I'm never, never sick at sea!*
Chorus:	*What, never?*
Captain:	*No, never!*
Chorus:	*What, never?*
Captain:	*Hardly ever!*

Get the message? Did you sing along as you read these lyrics? Don't you also wish that the changing from *never* to *hardly ever* just had to do with being sick at sea?

A friend of mine sent me a number of quotes that he feels are so prophetic and true that they apply to this time in our history. I would like to share a few of them:

If you don't read the newspaper you are uninformed; if you do read the newspaper, you are misinformed. Mark Twain

Suppose you were an idiot. And suppose you were a member of Congress.... But then I repeat myself. Mark Twain

I contend that for a nation to try to tax itself into prosperity is like a man standing in a bucket and trying to lift himself up by the handle. Winston Churchill

If you think health care is expensive now, wait until you see what it costs when it's free.
P. J. O'Rourke

Talk is cheap ... except when Congress does it. Unknown

What the country needs are more unemployed politicians. Edward Langley

A government big enough to give you everything you want, is strong enough to take everything you have. Thomas Jefferson

Most of these were written long ago, but are still right on today.

Be careful about using the word "never"
and be cautious of those who do.

22

CAREER

A Workplace Priority

Maybe you aren't as unhappy as you think.

Almost everyone gets upset or frustrated at work sometime during their working careers. It is natural and can be expected. It is important not to do something foolish when we are going through a trying time. The wise thing to do is analyze fully what is going on, evaluate your priorities and develop a plan of action.

The first part of the analysis should be to look at the job itself. Think about the different functions of the job. Make a list of all the actions and responsibilities that are associated with it, such as planning meetings, coaching, strategic planning, performance reviews, communicating, preparing presentations, studying, customer contacts, solving problems, personnel issues, preparing reports, long-range planning, and so forth.

You know there is a lot to every job and much that often is taken for granted. Interestingly, that is the case for both you and your boss. This is something to think about; take actions to assure that all you do is known and appreciated. Likewise, think about all that your boss does that goes unnoticed. Chances are he or she is not getting the recognition and appreciation that is deserved.

Considering all these different aspects of your job, how happy are you at work? Which parts of the job do you like and which don't you like? Do you feel motivated, challenged, appreciated and rewarded for your contributions? If you spend eight to twelve hours a day five days a week at work, shouldn't job happiness and satisfaction be a high priority for you?

Take time now to think about just how happy and motivated you are, and why. This is a subjective and personal evaluation that will, of course, vary from person to person. So I would suggest making a list of those aspects of your job that you like most. List the top ten things you like most about your job, where you work and the company.

Here is an example:

Things I Like Most about My Job

- I like the people with whom I work. (3)
- The company has a good reputation and is respected in the community. (8)
- I like the facility—it is clean, modern, safe, convenient and comfortable. (9)
- I like our products. (10)
- I like the amount of travel I do on business. (7)
- The benefits are okay. (6)
- The pay is okay. (5)
- I feel secure in my present position. (4)
- I feel I have opportunity for growth and advancement. (2)
- I feel I have a good future here and will not have to relocate. (1)

After you have completed the list, go back and review it to see if you have considered all parts of the job. Now, evaluate the list to rank these top ten in order of importance to you, with 1 being the most important and 10 being the least important. Rankings are shown on this list just as an example.

How many of the items from the above list are on your list? Should some of them be included, but are not because they don't fit your situation?

You might want to compile a similar list with ten things you don't like about your job. I would bet you have a much harder time listing ten things you don't like than the top ten that you do.

The overall analysis probably will lead to the conclusion that there are many more positives than negatives at your job. If this is so, focus on the positives and try to change the negatives in a productive and upbeat way.

Compliment someone at work for the good job they have done or are doing.

23

COMMITTING

It's Up to Me

Evaluate your attitude, performance and perceptions.

No matter how bad or how good things are at work, at your organization, or even at home, improvements can and should be made. Let's assume things now are about the same as they were the past year or even the past several years. If this is the case, you can be reasonably certain that things are not going to change all by themselves, are they?

This is underscored by "If it is to be, it is up to me." If you choose, and it would be a good idea to do so, you can add "with the help of God."

When considering making changes, it's a good idea to be a good scout and be prepared first. As an example, I have consulted companies and individuals within companies about the right time to increase prices to customers. The right time is when you have a need AND you are performing well with on-time deliveries, good quality and good communications. If you are having problems with an account, it's surely not the right time to ask for a price increase.

The same is true regarding asking your boss for a raise or consideration for promotion, or even making suggestions for improvements at the company. The right time is when you are doing more than what is expected, and the company knows it. It is when you are consistently on time with your reports or projects. It is when you know you have proven your worth. This makes sense, doesn't it?

So, my suggestion would be to do a personal evaluation of your attitude, your performance and how you think you're perceived by your leaders and your peers. Here is a key word—perceived. You know what you are doing, but how are you perceived by others? Here are some suggestions or questions to ask:

Personal Performance Questions

- Is your work schedule impressive or is it a problem? Do you arrive early and stay late? What about lunch and other breaks?

- Does your boss have to follow up on requests and assignments he gives you?
- Do you feel you are sometimes not included in discussions or meetings that you should be a part of?
- Do you do a good job of keeping management informed as to what you are doing?
- Do you know what "bugs" your boss or management? If so, do you ever bug them?
- Do you have the "right" company friends? Do you hang out with the right people?
- Do you frequently get involved in those negative discussions that unfortunately take place all too often?
- Do you think your boss or management likes you and likes to be around you?

Performance Improvement Suggestions

- When your boss asks you for bread, give him or her cake. Do more than what is expected. Make it more complete, more professional, and provide it earlier than requested.
- What hot buttons does your boss have? Don't fight these, even if you don't agree. Remember, he or she is the boss.
- What bugs your boss? Don't do anything that upsets your boss or management. What would be gained by doing such things?
- Be positive at all times. Don't enter into water cooler complaint sessions. I think there are ears in the water cooler.
- Communicate more often. Keep your boss well informed. Anticipate his or her needs for information and provide it.
- What can you do to make your boss more successful?
- Swallow your pride. Not a good thing to win an argument with a customer or with your boss. It is okay of course to voice your opinion if it is done in a positive way. Once done, then move on.
- Be kind to others in the organization. It shows and is the right thing to do.
- If there is a question of whether or not to do something, just do it!

Think about these actions and consider seriously doing those that are appropriate for you or others that you have added to this list.

When someone asks for bread, give them cake.

24

COMMUNICATING

The Written Word

The benefits of communicating in writing easily outweigh the negatives.

How many times have you wished you had something in writing? Or you thought, "Why didn't I put that in writing? I should have confirmed our discussion and our agreement."

In today's fast-paced society, so much of our communication is verbal, and often by voice mail messages. This leads to misunderstandings and assumptions that are, unfortunately, oftentimes not correct.

I believe this is the case for business discussions, organization meetings and decisions, and, yes, even for family planning and agreements. There are many benefits to communicating in writing. Some of the advantages of writing what you have to say are the following:

Advantages of Written Communication

- You can plan in advance what you want to communicate.
- You can review what you intend to send before sending it.
- You can solicit help in preparing your written message.
- You and the recipient will have a written record of what you communicated.
- Your communication can easily be shared with others.
- A picture (the written word) is worth a thousand words (verbal communication).

There are, however, also disadvantages of communicating in writing:

Disadvantages of Written Communication

- There is no immediate feedback with written communication.
- Negotiating in writing is extremely difficult.

- Your written communication could be shared with others whom you did not intend to see it.
- Your written communication might be misunderstood, and you won't know about it for some time, if ever.
- You may communicate better verbally than in writing. Be the best that you can be.
- You may not know when or where the reader will receive your written communication. Is timing critical?
- You have no control over the mood or attitude of the recipient when he or she receives your communication. Consider the effect of poor timing.
- You cannot make adjustments or changes based on the immediate reaction of the reader, as you could in face-to-face communication.
- If you have a competitor, consider how he is communicating to your prospect. Do a better job of communicating than the competitor.

Think of these advantages and disadvantages when deciding how and when to communicate. Consider the possibility of doing both. As an example, see or call the recipient prior to sending the written communication to explain what you are doing. Follow up shortly after it is received to see if there are any questions. Also remember you can easily confirm your verbal communication in writing after your face-to-face meeting.

Consider whether anything has happened within the last few days that should be confirmed or followed with a written note. If so, take the opportunity to "put it in writing."

25

COMMUNICATING

Put It in Writing

Other than lack of immediate feedback, it's effective.

The advantages and disadvantages of communicating in writing have been discussed in another *Actions Speak Louder* action. A few of the key advantages and disadvantages are as follows:

Advantages: You can plan in advance what you want to communicate. It can be reviewed, and both you and the recipient will have a written record. Good advantages.

Disadvantages: There is not immediate feedback with written communication. Your communication might be misunderstood or taken the wrong way, and you won't know about it for some time, if ever. You cannot make adjustments based on the immediate reaction of the reader, as you could in face-to-face communication. These disadvantages are important to consider.

Written communications are effective and many times necessary. This being the case, let's look at some suggestions for making written communication as positive and effective as possible.

Suggestions for Effective Written Communication

1. Think about who the reader or readers will be. What are their expectations? Your written communication probably will be shared, so quality is important.
2. Write in short, easy to understand sentences. Could there be more than one interpretation of what you are saying? Try reading it out loud. Or have someone else read it to see if it is clear without having to be reread.
3. Write to the reader. Use *you* often and *I* or *me* as little as possible. If you must, consider *we* rather than *I*.

4. Keep it simple. The front page of the Wall Street Journal and all of USA Today are written for the eighth-grade reading level. This is not the place to impress your reader with a fancy vocabulary. Clarity and understanding are the goals.

5. Know what you are communicating. Be accurate and truthful. Make sure you are right in what you are writing.

6. Write the same way you talk. It is you writing the letter, so be you.

7. Try not to be dull or boring. Add some excitement, paint vivid pictures, tell stories and be descriptive. Have fun writing—enjoy it. It is okay to have a sense of humor when writing.

8. Try to have a night to think about what you have written before you mail or send your communication.

9. Write and read extensively. This advice is from Stephen King, a prolific writer. If you want to be a good writer, you have to do two things—read a lot and write a lot. Makes sense, doesn't it?

10. Break it down. Where appropriate, use bullet points.

11. Keep paragraphs to no more than six lines. Short paragraphs encourage the reader to read all that is written.

12. Don't use all caps. They are harder to read and it gives the impression that you are shouting at the reader.

13. Don't use written communication to be critical, to share bad news, or to discuss a controversial issue. Do this in person.

14. Write letters to family and friends just for the fun of it. People save letters and delete e-mails.

15. Don't communicate in writing when you are mad, upset or tired. Also, don't send your communication to someone who might be mad, upset or tired.

16. Know exactly what should be communicated. Does your communication completely satisfy the objective? If there is any doubt, correct it so there is no doubt at all.

Consider starting written communication this week.

Practice written communication by writing a letter to a friend or family member.

26

COUNTRY

Under God

Red Skelton's 1969 commentary is worth revisiting.

The Fourth of July is over. Americans celebrated Independence Day in many ways.

Some of us spent time thinking about what it means to be an American and how blessed we are. Others probably didn't really give it a second thought, because we often take our freedom and liberty for granted.

Nearly everyone had the experience of seeing the American flag waving, and some recited the Pledge of Allegiance. The flag waving and hearing these famous words made me think of the late Red Skelton.

The following words were spoken by him on his television program, January 14, 1969. He related the story of his teacher, Mr. Laswell, who felt his students had come to think of the Pledge of Allegiance as merely something to recite in class each day.

Commentary on the Pledge of Allegiance
by Red Skelton

I've been listening to you boys and girls recite the Pledge of Allegiance all semester and it seems as though it is becoming monotonous to you. If I may, may I recite it and try to explain to you the meaning of each word?

I—me, an individual, a committee of one.
Pledge—dedicate all of my worldly goods to give without self-pity.
Allegiance—my love and my devotion.
To the flag—our standard, Old Glory, a symbol of Freedom; Wherever she waves there is respect, because your loyalty has given her a dignity that shouts, Freedom is everybody's job.
United—that means that we have all come together.

States—individual communities that have united into 48 great states. Forty-eight individual communities with pride and dignity and purpose; all divided with imaginary boundaries, yet united to a common purpose, and that is love for country.

And to the republic—*a state in which sovereign power is invested in representatives chosen by the people to govern. And government is the people; and it's from the people to the leaders, not from the leaders to the people.*

For which it stands, one nation—*meaning, so blessed by God.*

Indivisible—*incapable of being divided.*

With liberty—*which is freedom, the right of power to live one's own life without threats, fear, or some sort of retaliation.*

And justice—*the principle or quality of dealing fairly with others.*

For all—*which means, boys and girls, it's as much your country as it is mine.*

And now, boys and girls, let me hear you recite the Pledge of Allegiance:

'I pledge allegiance to the Flag of the United States of America, and to the Republic, for which it stands, one nation, indivisible, with liberty and justice for all.'

Red Skelton went on to say, "Since I was a small boy, two states have been added to our country, and two words have been added to the Pledge of Allegiance: **Under God.** Wouldn't it be a pity if someone said that is a prayer, and that it would be eliminated from schools, too"?

Wouldn't it be wonderful if all of our congressional leaders would read or listen to Red Skelton's "Commentary on the Pledge of Allegiance" and think about what this means today? With the approval rating of Congress at an all-time low of some 14%, don't you think our elected representatives would start looking at themselves and thinking, "Are we really doing the job we were elected to do?"

For instance, "And government is the people; and it's from the people to the leaders, not from the leaders to the people." Why isn't this happening?

There are three suggestions for this *Actions Speak Louder* action: First, encourage your representatives in congress to listen to Red Skelton's commentary; second, do whatever is necessary, whenever it is necessary, to battle the ACLU to keep **Under God** in the Pledge of Allegiance; third, think about the meaning of each of the words when reciting the Pledge of Allegiance.

Listen to Red Skelton's commentary on the website listed in this article.

27

Practice Good Judgment

Empowering employees equals customer satisfaction.

Nordstrom is probably one of the best department stores anywhere in providing outstanding customer service.

They empower their employees to do whatever is necessary to satisfy their customers. In fact, they want to do more than just satisfy their customers—they want to capture them. The employees are dedicated to thinking like the customer. This is a unique philosophy, but it shouldn't be.

Nordstrom is a Hall of Fame member on *Fortune Magazine's* "100 Best Companies to work for" list. Their 2007 rating was 24.

When new employees start with the company, they are given the employee manual—all one page of it. It is a simple 5½ by 7½ inch card that is two-sided and says:

> *Welcome to Nordstrom*
>
> *We're glad to have you with our company.*
> *Our number one goal is to provide*
> *outstanding customer service. Set both*
> *your personal and professional goals high.*
> *We have great confidence in your ability to achieve them.*
> *Our employee handbook is simple.*
>
> *We have only one rule ...*

> *Our only rule ...*
> **Use good judgment in**
> **All situations.**

I read about one manager who explains this in a simple way. He said the two key things at Nordstrom are the following:

1. Don't steal from us
2. Don't chew gum

This does require a little explanation. I believe these two statements mean more than these seven small words seem to say:

The first, "Don't steal from us," I believe means you are empowered to do your job in a way that provides outstanding customer service. You are paid to do this and are rewarded for the results. If you don't do this, you are stealing from the company and its reputation.

If you are not using your time wisely, or are not giving it your all with customers, you are stealing from yourself, your company and your customers. This is stealing.

The second, "Don't chew gum," means what you would think. It is not professional to chew gum in public, so chewing gum represents not being professional or not being the best that you can be. It is probably more effective to use this simple reference than to tell employees how to dress, what their posture should be, and so forth. When they are told not to chew gum, I would assume they would get the picture.

The only rule—"Use good judgment in all situations"—is really not as totally empowering to employees as it would sound. Why? Because it would not be using good judgment to commit to something that was not reasonable and not in the best interests of the company—even for one that seriously wants outstanding customer service.

In our everyday life, personally and in business, what can we learn from Nordstrom? I think the most important lesson is to put a high priority on practicing the use of good judgment. But how can we be encouraged to use good judgment? Is it something that can be taught?

Consider the following analysis: How do you learn good judgment? The answer is—learning from your mistakes. Why do you make mistakes? Because you used poor judgment. Is this kind of a vicious circle?

Learning from our mistakes, and not making them again, would show good judgment. Learning from the mistakes of others would also show good judgment. So would taking a second look at decisions we make before action is taken. I believe thinking about who is going to be affected is important in exercising good judgment.

There are many, many opportunities available to all of us in any number of areas. Using Nordstrom's example, we would use good judgment in all situations, we would not steal from ourselves and we would not chew gum.

Practice good judgment and compliment those who demonstrate good judgment.

28

COUNTRY

Old-Time Values

Be proud of your friends.

Are there old-time values that are still around today, or have today's new values taken over our country? I think this is an important subject to think about. Some may want to take a more active role in leading the return of old-time, traditional values.

A number of years ago, Dean Martin had John Wayne as a guest on his television program. Both were riding horses—Dean looked out of place on his horse, and "Duke" looked right at home. Here is what they had to say to each other:

Dean: "Duke, you have a new daughter and are one of the most successful actors in the world. What do you want for your daughter?" John Wayne said, "Well, same as any parent, I guess. I want to stick around long enough to see that she gets started right.

"I would like her to know some of the values that we knew as kids, some of those values that too many people these days are thinking old fashioned.

"Most of all, I want her to be grateful, as I am every day of my life, to be living in these United States.

"I know it might sound a little corny, but the first thing my daughter is learning from me is the Lord's Prayer and some of the Psalms.

"I don't care if she memorizes the Gettysburg Address, just so long as she understands it. And since little girls are seldom called upon to defend our country, she may never have to raise her hand for that call, but I certainly want her to respect all those who do. That's what I want for my daughter."

Dean Martin closed with "I'm proud to know you, Duke."

Doesn't that closing sound great? I'm proud to know you. Perhaps it takes believing in the old-time values and doing as you believe to have people say, "I'm proud to know you."

Interesting—the Lord's Prayer and the Gettysburg Address. Christians know the Lord's Prayer, of course, and know that it is as timely today as it was 2,000 years ago, but what about the Gettysburg Address? Is it also timely today? I would say most definitely, yes. Read through it again and substitute war against extreme Islamic terrorists for the Civil War.

The Gettysburg Address
November 19, 1863, Gettysburg, Pennsylvania

Four score and seven years ago our fathers brought forth on this continent a new nation, conceived in Liberty, and dedicated to the proposition that all men are created equal.

Now we are engaged in a great civil war, testing whether that nation, or any nation, so conceived and so dedicated, can long endure. We are met on a great battle-field of that war. We have come to dedicate a portion of that field, as a final resting place for those who here gave their lives that that nation might live. It is altogether fitting and proper that we should do this.

But, in a larger sense, we can not dedicate ... we can not consecrate ... we can not hallow this ground. The brave men, living and dead, who struggled here, have consecrated it, far above our poor power to add or detract. The world will little note, nor long remember what we say here, but it can never forget what they did here. It is for us the living, rather, to be dedicated here to the unfinished work which they who fought here have thus far so nobly advanced. It is rather for us to be here dedicated to the great task remaining before us ... that from these honored dead we take increased devotion to that cause for which they gave the last full measure of devotion ... that we here highly resolve that these dead shall not have died in vain ... that this nation, under God, shall have a new birth of freedom ... and that government of the people, by the people, for the people, shall not perish from the earth.

Thank you, Abraham Lincoln, for this timely message to all of us.

If you are proud to know someone, tell them so, and add that you're proud to have them as a friend.

29

CARING

Make Your Own Fun

Decide to have fun and make it happen.

We spent spring break in Mexico with our kids and grandkids from Chicago. They were especially excited about getting some sun and warm weather because they had left snow and cold weather. It had been a long winter for them. You know, up north the sun doesn't seem to shine very often during the winter months, and it gets pretty depressing. So, going to the beaches in Mexico in March/April is a real getaway.

It was great being together, and as usual, we learned much from our grandkids. The first day they arrived, our daughter-in-law asked Cole (13) how he felt about the pools and beaches. His answer was, "Great, but we will have to make our own fun."

During the first afternoon there, Cole hadn't seen all the activities that were available where we were staying, but it didn't matter, because they were willing and able to make their own fun.

They played catch in the pool, games on a water raft, king of the mountain on a sand dune in the ocean, jump or dive games, water tag and others for hours.

This made quite an impression on me, and made me think back to our vacation times with our family, when our kids were the ages of our grandkids today. We also made our own fun and usually with simple things. We didn't spend time with elaborate electronic games and devices. We made our own fun with what was available, such as pails and shovels to make things out of sand. And there were always balls for playing games.

In the neighborhood, we played all kinds of pick-up games, ranging from baseball to kick-the-can to simple hide-and-seek games. These were not planned by the parents or organizations; the kids made their own fun. The only problem here was deciding who was picked first and who was picked last for each team. Somehow, it always seemed to work out without feelings being hurt, or at least that's what we thought.

What we learned or relearned from the grandkids on that trip is that it is up to us to make our own fun, and we can do it. Just think about how much fun it is to be together and to share with each other your thoughts, your ambitions, your experiences, as well as your worries or concerns. It also made us think about how very important it is to plan to have fun in our lives and to do it every day. It just takes a little planning, desire and the right attitude to make it happen. We should make sure this happens, because what can be more fun than having fun?

What is fun? Fun is different for each of us. Fun for you might be traveling, entertaining, playing musical instruments, singing, reading, leisure time, working out, watching sporting events or just being together with family and friends. For others, fun might be just having some private quiet time for thinking.

Whatever is most fun for you and your family should be included in your planning process and scheduling each and every day. Are you doing this now? If you are not making time for your own fun, ask yourself why not. The answer is very likely that you are too busy, or you have other priorities, or you have just not thought about making your own fun plan a reality.

Fun should also be included in the workplace. At ABB, we had seven Guiding Principles that we published and promoted. My favorite two are as follows:

- *Providing a working environment that fosters personal commitment, genuine teamwork, innovation and true employee empowerment.*
- *Sharing good times with employees, customers and suppliers.*

The last probably made the biggest impression on our customers—that we wanted to share good times with them. You see, we were making our own fun for our employees, customers and suppliers.

Make your own fun a regular part of your life.

30

Can Instant Replay Work?

Is instant replay only for sports?

The 2008 Wimbledon men's final was a tremendous match. During the final set it looked like either player could win. It was exciting up to the final point. Rafael Nadal beat David Ferrer in five sets. I think the challenge system, or instant replay technology, proved that it does belong on the tennis courts as well as other athletic fields and courts. I don't know if instant replay helped one player or the other, but it did eliminate speculation about bad calls.

During all the men's singles at Wimbledon, there were 224 challenges, with 64 correct challenges and 160 incorrect challenges. Rafael Nadal had 22 challenges, with 9 being overturned. David Ferrer had 8 challenges, with 3 overturned. That is about 40%. The goal is to have 100% correct calls, which is almost impossible with calls being made by people. Correct calls in any sport are important, and therein lies the real value of having instant replay.

Perhaps one of the first times instant replay was used to review an official's call in sports involved Wichita Falls' Denny Bishop. In the late '70s, Denny was officiating a basketball game in Fayetteville, Arkansas, with Baylor playing Arkansas. On one play, Denny had to make three decisions—was there a foul, was there basket interference, and was the basket good? He made what he believed was a correct call, but one of the coaches challenged it. Denny happened to notice that a local television station was telecasting the game. He asked the TV crew if they could rerun the play; they said they could. Both coaches wanted to know what he was doing. He answered that he wanted to make sure his call was correct. The replay showed that his call was right.

The local news media made a big deal of this "instant replay." The Dallas Cowboys even called Denny to ask how it worked. As you might imagine, the Southwest Conference also called Denny to ask him about his using instant replay, because there was nothing in the rule book that allowed such a review. Denny again said that all he wanted to do was to make the correct call. The Southwest Conference asked him not to do it again.

Instant replay was first adopted by the NFL in a limited instant replay system in 1986. The system was a failure and was abandoned in 1991. The current system began in 1999 with improvements to shorten the time for officials to review the plays; it also allowed the opportunity to challenge field calls.

College football instant replay for reviews started in the 2004 season, experimentally, in the Big Ten Conference. In the 2005 season, all conferences were allowed to use instant replay.

Basketball uses instant replay primarily for time questions, such as whether the shot was released before time expired, or to determine if the shot was a two-point or a three-point field goal. This seems to work well for all levels of basketball.

And now, Major League Baseball is considering using instant replay. They are saying that instant replay is needed because there have been so many blown calls this year. Can you imagine doing anything at the old ball park that might slow down the game? You do want the right calls made, but baseball needs to speed up the game and reduce the waiting time, not lengthen it.

Instant replay review should be used to make sure the call is correct. Instant replay is needed in politics. Politicians should have their views on issues recorded, and every time they change their policies or views on an issue, the instant replay should automatically be shown. Then the politician would have to say which one is correct.

The reason for this would be to ensure that the politician would select which position he or she truly believes in and would stick with when in office. Otherwise, how will we know what each politician (candidate) will do if elected? If we can't get instant replay in politics, then how about asking for honesty?

Take the time to let those running for public office know how important honesty is to you.

31

COMMUNICATING

Talk to Me

It's okay to call for a time-out.

Have you been in meetings, either as a member of an organization or as an employee of a company, in which the boss or chairman of the committee surprises you with questions that put you on the spot? Or a company is meeting with a client or customer, and there are questions asked or comments made that are out of place? They shouldn't be made without prior internal discussions and planning. Unfortunately, this happens all too often and generally is due to a few basic practices not being followed.

These are some of the reasons why this happens in meetings:

- Lack of proper communication
- Lack of adequate planning
- An ego problem
- Forgetting the Golden Rule

Here are some suggestions for avoiding this embarrassing and unprofessional situation of the team not looking and acting like a team:

1. Always, always have a planning meeting with all individuals involved to discuss what will be covered and to understand clearly who will be doing what.
2. Anticipate the questions and concerns the client, customer, supplier or other department might have, and be prepared with the right answers. Know in advance who will answer each question.
3. Review minutes of past meetings to ensure that all commitments have been met, or at least have answers for what has happened or will happen.
4. Consider the individuals with whom you will be meeting, and decide if there are special needs that should be addressed during the meeting.

5. If you have a supervisor or boss who likes to put his subordinates on the spot in meetings to show how "tough" he is, suggest you have a meeting before the customer meeting to ensure all bases are covered. If the boss doesn't think this is necessary, go ahead and meet with the other members of the team to make sure you are all prepared.

6. Know that it is okay to stand up for each other during this planning meeting. The purpose is to have a well-prepared meeting and not to be hurtful of anyone on the team or on the customer's team.

7. Put the planning information in writing for all the members of the team. Make sure those who weren't able to attend the meeting are brought up to speed.

8. Be considerate and kind. Remember the Golden Rule.

During any meeting, it is possible for things not to be going the way you had planned and wanted. The important thing is to recognize this is happening and to simply call for a time-out. It is absolutely okay to tell your customer or supplier that you want to take a time-out break to give both you and them some time to discuss the situation. This can be done in a very positive and professional way. The customer probably is looking for an opportunity to be alone as well.

One time, we were meeting with a potential customer who was very insistent on having two special features in our product. We were in serious negotiations and knew these two features were not necessary for this product line to be successful. They were not budging, and neither were we, because we felt we were right. I'm sure they felt they were right too. We called for a time-out, and within about 15 minutes, we decided it was foolish to fight them as to who was right and who was wrong. We decided to make the changes they asked for, because it was as much a matter of pride as cost. And as the story goes, we lived happily every after. Incidentally, they dropped these two features within two years.

The point is that without a time-out and some simple common sense, we would have won the battle and lost the war. As it turned out, it was a win-win situation for both sides, and isn't that what you are always looking for through good communication, good planning, and using the Golden Rule?

Remember the "Golden Rule" in conducting meetings.

32

COMMUNICATING

Time to Bring in S.W.O.T.

Communication is the key to happy relationships.

One of the main reasons for divorce is poor communication. Many say it is finances, but at the heart of the financial problem is very likely poor communication. So, if poor communication isn't the top reason for couples splitting up, it surely is right up there.

Everyone knows the three rules of real estate success—location, location, location. In business, the three rules of success are communication, communication, communication. In a happy and successful marriage, the three rules must also be communication, communication, communication.

Several weeks ago, I was talking to a friend who is CEO of his own company. He had just recently completed a three-day retreat doing strategic planning with his management team. He is a good leader and a good communicator. Guess what turned out to be the biggest need within his company. He was surprised to find it was communication. He had no idea his employees felt out of the communication loop. Across the board, the employees wanted better two-way communication.

I was involved with a company helping with strategic planning and conducting what is called a S.W.O.T (strengths, weaknesses, opportunities, threats) analysis. The purpose of the analysis was to have the management team agree on where the company is today. This means listing the strengths and weaknesses in an order of importance. Once the strengths and weaknesses are accepted, the next step is to look for opportunities to take advantage of the strengths and to correct or improve the weaknesses. It is also valuable to look at possible threats, so that a "what if" scenario can be developed.

With this company, communication was the number-one weakness, and interestingly enough, also the number-one opportunity. It is interesting, but shouldn't be a surprise. With most companies, the employees are crying for better communication. It isn't increased pay that is the main problem; it is two-way communication between management and employees.

What communication do employees want?

First, the employees want to know where the co
to know the vision for the company, and they war
The vision should tell the employees what kind of
build. Where is the company going? The mission s
purpose of the business?

Employees should know the core values of the m
how decisions will be made and how employees and

For communication of the company's vision, missi
they must be real. They must be lived. They must be be
on a plaque in the reception room.

Employees want to know how they are doing. Go
than an annual review. Regular mentoring, coaching, f
requested by all employees, lead to successful employe

One very good way to improve company communi
around." This works if the manager spends a certain
around the facility. To be effective in this managemen
It can't be forced or awkward. If it isn't natural at fii
have a purpose for visiting with a few employees. Then

Good communication is a two-way street, whethe
means being a good listener. Focus on listening first ar

What is exciting about communication's being be
terrific opportunity is that it costs nothing to move fro
it takes is desire, awareness, caring, commitment, fo
required—in a marriage or in a business.

Focus on listening and
communication.

Pro

Just think

Yes, I'm pro
proud of our
were some dis
performances
watched with

The basket
donnas. You
their country
won much m
and here in t
we are proud

So many o
the track star
Bryan Clay w
winner is co
distinction.
others on the

Michael P
years. The 40
over and ove

And how
How proud
problem wit
like this fror
All this m

COUNTRY

ud to Be an American

about our Olympics.

ud to be an American. After watching two weeks of the Olympics, I am very
thletes, how they performed and how they conducted themselves. There
ppointments, such as dropped batons, but there were many unbelievable
and results that more than offset the disappointments. The whole country
excitement and, most definitely, with pride.

all team played together as a team, not as a bunch of highly-paid prima
ould tell it meant a lot to all of them to be on the team and to represent
They played hard and they deserved to win the gold medal. I think they
re than the gold; they won the respect of a lot of people around the world
e United States. They played with the heart of Americans, and that is why
of them.

her individuals and teams were outstanding. The swimmers, the gymnasts,
, the volleyball players, and so many others who gave us reason to celebrate.
on the men's decathlon. This is quite an honor, because the decathlon
sidered the best athlete in the world. We are proud an American won this
e women gymnasts showed such class and seemed to really care about the
r team and those against whom they competed.

elps is, of course, Michael Phelps, and he will be remembered for years and
-meter free relay and the 100-meter butterfly finals will continue to be shown
and over. How could he possibly have won gold medals in those two events?
bout Dara Torres, who, as a 41-year-old swimmer, won two silver medals?
f her were you when she held up her race because one swimmer had a
her swimsuit and might have missed the race? You would expect something
an American. That's the way we are.

de me think of Lee Greenwood's "Proud to be an American":

I'd thank my lucky stars,
to be livin here today.
'Cause the flag still stands for freedom,
and they can't take that away.

And I'm proud to be an American,
where at least I know I'm free.
And I won't forget the men who died,
who gave that right to me.

And I gladly stand up,
next to you and defend her still today.
'Cause there ain't no doubt I love this land,
God bless the USA.

After the Olympics, did you have withdrawal symptoms? Does it help that we moved from the Olympics to Denver and Minneapolis/Saint Paul for political conventions, where many didn't act as though they were proud of our country? I guess political speeches are supposed to motivate the voters by saying bad things about the other party and their candidates. Is it effective to talk about how terrible conditions are in our country? Somehow, this just doesn't seem right. We are living in the best country in the world. We should be proud of our way of life, our people, our freedoms, our opportunities, our heritage and our many blessings. So, why do politicians have to be so negative about what makes us so great? Is this the right way to win elections?

Democrats and Republicans should step back, think about the Olympics, our national pride, and together sing loudly and with gusto, "I'm proud to be an American. 'Cause there ain't no doubt I love this land, God bless the USA."

 Show your pride in America by your words and your actions.

34

Happiness at Work

Accentuate the positive; eliminate the negative.

Is the glass half full, or half empty? Is the sun about to shine, or is it about to storm? Are we going to make our plan, or are we going to fall short? Is he going to get a hit, or strike out? Are we going to get the order, or lose it because of price or some other reason? Is our stock going to go up, or go down over time?

Are you an optimist, or pessimist, or generally optimistic, or naturally pessimistic? The optimist will look for the bright side of life and for the positive aspects of the job most of the time, while the pessimist will be thinking about the job in a negative or critical way much of the time. Being one or the other can make a big difference in how the job is viewed.

There are many employee satisfaction surveys conducted that generally list about the same likes and dislikes. The following are the top five things most liked about a typical company from a typical survey:

1.   I feel I have a good future here and will not have to relocate.
2.   I feel I have opportunity for growth and advancement.
3.   I like the people I work with.
4.   I feel secure in my present position.
5.   The pay is okay.

Think about these five as an example. This person feels he or she has opportunity, a good future, likes the people he or she works with, is secure and the pay is okay. Hardly anyone is going to say the pay is great. Pay being okay is okay. So, really what more could anyone ask for?

What about your list? Are the top five as positive and strong as these, or are they even better? That's great if this is so. If not, there are choices for improvement that we will discuss later on. For discussion's sake, let's say they are positive. So, what do we do next?

We "accentuate the positive, eliminate the negative, latch on to the affirmative, and don't mess with Mister In-Between." This means we focus and concentrate on the positive aspects of the job. We work to eliminate the negatives. And we don't waste time on those who really don't matter (Mister In-Between).

The next exercise is to list those areas or items that you would like to see changed or improved for the success of the company and the happiness and improved morale of the employees. Make a list of five to seven items to improve. The following are examples:

Things I Would Like to See Improved or Changed in Our Company

- Improve communication within the company. We need to hear more from top management.
- It would be helpful to have a better vision as to where the company is going.
- Better performance reviews. I would like to know more about future opportunities. How well am I doing? What can I do better? How can I improve my job performance?
- I would like to see more team-building and better communication between departments.
- I think it would be helpful if we could all be working toward the same common goals.

It's very interesting to note that all these areas for improvement basically have a lot to do with communication. This is the real world, and improved communication is probably the number-one need in business.

Is your list of things you like about the company and things you would like to see changed very different from these items? Doesn't it make sense to accentuate the positive things you like about the company and work to eliminate or improve the negatives? Consider preparing your own personal plan to do just that—accentuate the positives and eliminate the negatives. You will probably be amazed at what a difference it will make in your work environment and in those with whom you work. Give it a try.

Ask someone at work for their advice on a project you are working on or a problem you are struggling with. They will appreciate being asked, and you might get some very good help.

35

CARING

Act Kindly

Kindness spreads as the receiver is motivated to pass it on.

How often do you see others performing little acts of kindness? It's happening all the time, but generally these acts are being done in modest ways that don't draw attention to the one being kind.

Some refer to these acts as random acts of kindness. They are called this because these special acts often happen in a random way—they are not planned. They just happen because the opportunity is there for someone to perform a kind act, and action is taken.

Little acts of kindness can become big acts. They become big acts because kindness generates kindness. It has a way of growing and spreading as each kindness receiver is motivated to also participate in little acts of kindness for others.

Kindness really is contagious. Let's just imagine what would happen if everyone performed a little act of kindness every week ... or what about every day? What a different world this would be.

I really enjoy reading or hearing quotations about almost any subject. This subject, little acts of kindness, is no exception. There are good reminders of what we should be thinking and doing. Here are a few quotations about kindness:

Kindness is a language which the deaf can hear and the blind can read. Mark Twain

Change the world one act of kindness at a time. Remember, our kindness is our power. Maribel

One can pay back the loan of gold, but one lies forever in debt to those who are kind. Malaysian Proverb

Kindness is free, so why not give some out? Lisandra Piercey

Kind words can be short and easy to speak, but their echoes are truly endless.
Mother Teresa

You cannot do a kindness too soon, for you never know how soon it will be too late.
Ralph Waldo Emerson

Man is honored for his wisdom, loved for his kindness. S. Cohen

I expect to pass through this world but once. Any good, therefore, that I can do or any kindness I can show to any fellow creature, let me do it now. Let me not defer or neglect it for I shall not pass this way again. Stephen Grellet

Don't wait for people to be kind, show them how. Author Unknown

When I was young, I admired clever people. Now that I am old, I admire kind people.
Abraham Joshua Heschel

The smallest good deed is better than the grandest good intention. Duquet

Have you had a kindness shown? Pass it on, 'Twas not given for thee alone, Pass it on; Let it travel down the years, Let it wipe another's tears, Till in Heaven the deed appears, Pass it on. Henry Burton

How can we make performing little acts of kindness a regular part of our everyday life? I know for many people it already is a high priority in their lives, and for others, maybe not so high. It might just be a question of awareness and realizing how important kindness can be in increasing happiness in many lives, including our own.

 Perform a little act of kindness today.

36

⊚〓⊚〓⊚〓 **CARING** ⊚〓⊚〓⊚

Say Something Nice ... and Really Mean It

It's amazing what a little praise can do.

A few summers ago, I watched a father trying to talk his teen-age son into jumping off a cliff into Possum Kingdom Lake. It wasn't a very high cliff and the boy wasn't a little kid; he was between his freshman and sophomore year in high school. He was a big boy, and from what the father said, I could tell he wanted his son to be a football player. It was surprising that a boy of the son's age had never dived, or much less jumped, into a lake from that height before.

The father said some really mean things to his son, trying to get him to be more courageous. He even called him a sissy and a little girl, and asked how in the world he expected to make the football team if he was afraid of just jumping into the lake.

The boy came down from the cliff without making the jump. The father kept on criticizing him—even had him crying. What do you think this did for the boy's self-esteem? How bad would any boy feel with his father belittling him in front of his own friends and strangers? I'll bet the boy never forgets that day. I was just a spectator, and I haven't forgotten it.

You wonder if this father ever gave any praise to his son, or if he was always critical about everything he did. If his son had been accustomed to receiving praise and had been positively supported and encouraged by his dad at the lake that day, no doubt he would have jumped. Then they could have celebrated together, and what good memories they would have had to share in the future.

One of the most positive motivational tools we all have is our ability to provide praise for others. Everyone wants to hear how well they are doing and how important they are to the organization, or even the family. There is, however, good praise and bad praise. Obviously, the goal is always to give good praise. Bad praise is probably worse than no praise at all.

Ingredients of good praise should include at least four elements:

1. Good praise should be timely. It should be given immediately after the event or behavior.
2. Good praise is sincere and personalized for the person being praised. It is okay to praise a group at the same time, but the individual should know clearly that the appreciation is specifically for him or her.
3. Good praise should describe specifically what you liked. It should not be just general, vague words of praise.
4. Good praise should not be given and then taken away. This means, don't praise someone as a way to lead into criticism. An example of this would be to say to someone, "You gave a very good, interesting talk, but shouldn't you have used more visual aids to help make your point?"

Being insincere, choosing a bad time, or making the praise conditional will turn it from good to bad, and the results from positive to negative.

Ken Blanchard in his *One Minute Manager* identifies seven steps for effective "One Minute Praising":

1. Tell people up front that you are going to let them know how they are doing.
2. Praise people immediately.
3. Tell people what they did right—be specific.
4. Tell people how good you feel about what they did right, and how it helps the organization and the other people who work there.
5. Stop for a moment of silence to let them "feel" how good you feel.
6. Encourage them to do more of the same.
7. Shake hands or touch people in a way that makes it clear that you support their success.

Since praise can be such a positive way of recognizing individuals and their good accomplishments, wouldn't it be a great idea for all of us to be looking for opportunities to praise our friends, family members and associates?

Seek opportunities to provide praise in the right way.

37

CAREER

Under Review

Annual evaluations are not a walk in the park for some.

Oh, no, is it performance review time again?

Whether it is for your job, your organization, or whether you are the reviewer or reviewee, you probably are willing to admit you don't look forward to this annual process. I think there are many reasons for this:

- Usually, the performance review is tied in with salary discussions, and, generally, these are not very positive.
- It is difficult to analyze performance over a year, and talk about it for an hour.
- Sometimes, the person doing the performance review really doesn't fully know what all the reviewee has done during the past year—good or bad.
- It is not our nature to talk about personal problems or areas in which the individual is weak, so we try to avoid these kinds of discussions. It also is not natural to talk about our own performance.
- The reviewer most likely is not in a position to make commitments to the reviewee concerning future advancements or salary increase if there is improved performance.
- Maybe the performance review process is outdated and doesn't address today's needs.
- It takes a great deal of time to prepare and conduct the performance review. Finding the time to do it right is difficult when it is not high on your priority list.
- Both individuals might be nervous about the review because of inadequate knowledge or preparation.
- Maybe there is a question of how secure both parties feel in their present positions.
- There might be concern about the company's downsizing or letting people go, and the review time might bring this out.
- It could be that something not good happened recently, and there is the fear that this one incident could affect the entire year's performance evaluation.

You might have other reasons why performance reviews are dreaded by many, including yourself. If so, why don't you add them to this list?

There are many things that can be done to overcome the negative feeling about performance reviews. Another *Actions Speak Louder* action—"How are you doing"?—will provide some suggestions to make the reviews much more positive.

Consider spending some time thinking about your own situation as the reviewee. Some things to think about:

- How would you rate your performance over the last year?
- Do you think there have been positive or negative changes since your last review?
- How do you think your boss would rate you now? Not how would you want him to rate you, but how is your performance perceived by your boss? Again, notice the use of the word "perceived."
- Write down what you are working for at your company. What are your goals? What job or jobs do you want next? What is your ultimate goal?
- Honestly and realistically speaking, do you have the dedication and determination necessary to reach these goals? Do you have the ability, and will you have the experience, to make these goals become a reality?
- What is your timetable for these things to happen?

Be honest with yourself.

 If your boss or someone else at work is doing an especially good job, congratulate them. Send a copy of your congratulations to the person's boss. Why not send a copy to your boss also?

38

COMMUNICATING

Two-Way Street

Effective communication takes initiative on your part.

When I was a young salesman in Boston, I thought I had all the answers and didn't need help from my boss, the district sales manager.

I guess I was somewhat independent and liked making the sale or breaking into a new account all on my own. Maybe because of this, we didn't have very good communication.

Because I was the youngest and newest salesman in the office, I was quite often assigned to take the visiting regional manager with me on sales calls. Others didn't want to do it. What I discovered while making calls with Joe Simon was that I really did like him and that he was able to say things and do things at accounts that I hadn't thought of. He really did help me.

Mainly, he helped me to understand that communication with management is very important and beneficial. It should not be looked at as a threat or a bad thing.

Gradually, I started spending more time with my district manager, and guess what! I found I really liked him, too, and he had knowledge and experience that I could use with my accounts. Our communication improved and so did my sales results.

I would bet that many who took the time to list things they would like to see changed at their job included communication with their boss or management. In most businesses, or within many organizations and even within some families, there are numerous opportunities for improving communication.

The lack of good communication in all these areas can result in misunderstandings, confusion and poor productivity.

Communication is definitely a two-way street. If you feel you are not having good communication with someone, think about taking the initiative to fix it rather than to blame the other party. Remember: "If it is to be, it is up to me."

So, how do we go about fixing (or improving) the communication at your job, organization or family? First, I think it would be good to understand and accept that communication is a two-way street, but the effort to improve it doesn't have to be a 50/50 deal. Why not start out by saying it is going to begin as a 90/10 kind of deal? That means you are going to do way more than the other party ... if it is to be.

Some suggestions for improving communications:

- Develop a plan that grows over time. Don't bombard the other person with lots and lots of communications from day one.
- Decide what the other person needs to know about what you or your department is doing.
- Make a list of all regular communications that are required in your job and when they are due. Plan to provide these communications consistently early in the future.
- Invite and involve the other person in your meetings or discussions.
- Ask him or her for advice on something you are working on. Remember to be a good listener. Thank him or her for the input and try to use it in some way.
- Make sure to introduce your boss to visitors and customers, and introduce him as your boss.
- Discuss performance reviews with your boss before you give them to your employees, if you are in this kind of position. This is a good way to find out what he or she thinks.
- Find out what kind of information your boss has to provide to his or her boss. Try to provide interesting and creative information that your boss can use in reporting.
- Focus on personal, face-to-face communications rather than e-mails.
- After a reasonable time, plan to have some kind of communication with your boss every day, every other day, or whatever is appropriate. Make it a regular part of your job.
- Understand that not all communication with your boss has to be heavy or revolve around some kind of problem. Make some discussions fun and enjoyable.
- When having discussions with your boss (or anyone else), give him or her your complete attention. Stop what you are doing and physically and mentally move into their space.

You know your situation, so add to this list what should be most effective for you. If these things are done, the communication definitely will improve, and you will see a movement closer to a 50/50 kind of deal.

Ask your boss for his advice or opinion on something you are working on when he or she doesn't expect it.

39

CULTIVATE CHARACTER

Take the High Road

Life is a journey.

Many think of life as a journey with numerous roads to choose from as one travels hour by hour, day by day, week by week and into the future. As a youth, the roads are not so long, but they can have bumps, and there is always the possibility of accidents and wrong turns. Some roads are safe, smooth, and all turns seem to be made in the right direction; then for seemingly no reason at all, the road conditions change.

The street signs sometimes are not very clear. And the distances from point to point seem to change at the wrong times. It is also hard to read and understand the maps we are given for directions. Sometimes the maps are clear and sometimes they are blurry. And they are always hard to fold.

Some people think the roads and their travels are scenic and full of adventure, with cool breezes in their faces and the sun always shining. Other people who travel the same roads don't see the beautiful scenery; they say that it's overcast during their journey. How can that be? Could it be that the expectations are different? Is it possible to see what you want to see and not see what you don't want to see?

Generally, parents tell or advise their children which roads to take and provide good directions. Many of us have difficulty accepting directions and understanding which roads to take.

First of all, it's hard to listen to directions and remember what was actually said. Also, there is oftentimes peer pressure suggesting different and more exciting roads to take. Someone is always trying to pass out different maps with different roads and directions showing the way.

Getting to a certain destination frequently seems to have both an easy and a difficult road. But why is it that the sure way of getting there is usually by a difficult road, requiring working along the way? The easy road is more appealing, and yet there are no assurances that it actually leads to the right destination. The easy road is riskier and the chances of getting lost are much greater. The maps say the choice is yours to make.

As we grow older, it becomes more obvious that good road maps are very important. It also is important to get the maps from the right sources. Where were they printed and by whom?

The right maps are necessary for success in journeying through life. Planning, setting goals, and establishing priorities are road maps that are used to chart the roads to take for health and happiness. These maps should show **dedication** and **determination** clearly and in bold letters.

Many motivational or spiritual books give advice on how to look at the maps you have been using and those you are planning to use for future journeys. The maps that seem to be the clearest are those that focus on establishing the top priorities in life and taking the right directions/actions that support those priorities. Changing maps is okay if you need to change directions.

Can you picture Robert Frost in 1920 looking at his map that showed two roads? He made a decision, of course; the following is the last stanza of his famous work:

"The Road Not Taken"

I shall be telling this with a sigh
Somewhere ages and ages hence:
Two roads diverged in a wood, and I—
I took the one less traveled by,
And that has made all the difference.

Use a map to highlight the most enjoyable places you have visited and add those places you want to go. Then make it happen.

40

CULTIVATE CHARACTER

Good Grammar and Good Manners

To be successful in your career, master them equally.

The other day, I said, "thank you" to a waiter, and he said, "no problem." I could easily tell that it was not a problem, but what I expected to hear was "you're welcome," not "no problem." What has happened to responses like thank you, please, excuse me, you're welcome and other expressions that are simple, polite, easily understood and appreciated?

We were in an elevator when a young man stepped out ahead of women who were waiting to exit. I suspect he had never been told this was not using good manners. Women should go first. One would think that the young man had observed this many times and would have known better.

I held the door open for a woman recently, and she didn't acknowledge me or say thank you. I didn't expect a tip, because I'm not a doorman, but a smile and thanks would have been nice. I have also witnessed, many times, men entering or leaving a building or room without holding the door open for others, including women.

Everyday I hear "me and Roger." I even hear this on radio talk shows. Is it easier to say "me and Roger" than "Roger and I"? I don't think so. Doesn't it just grate on your nerves and don't you feel like saying, "Don't you mean Roger and I"?

Good grammar and good manners are so very important in business and in everyday life. To be successful, I believe good manners and good grammar are necessary. Therefore, I think we should use dedication and determination to focus on improving grammar and manners. These are just subtle reminders of what we already know.

Good manners involve much more than opening doors, leaving the elevator after women have exited, and standing when a woman enters the room. Here are a few examples of practicing good manners:

- Listening in the right way. Being sincerely interested in others, learning their names and encouraging them to talk about themselves makes a good first impression when you meet someone.
- Avoiding criticizing others or regularly complaining about circumstances. The same goes for being negative or being a gossip. Be kind and positive.
- Being on time. It is proper and right to be a few minutes early for an appointment or meeting, but it is not proper to arrive early for a social engagement.
- Treating others as you would want to be treated. It is always good manners to think of others first. This is the Golden Rule of Manners.
- Giving compliments and accepting compliments in the right way. A simple thank you is probably the best way to acknowledge a compliment.
- Being aware of the circumstances and acting appropriately. For a man, this means such things as standing when a woman enters the room, leaves a table or comes to the table; opening doors; walking on the outside closest to the street; and not starting to eat until the hostess begins.
- Encouraging family and friends to make suggestions to improve your grammar and manners.
- Saying thank you. Consider sending thank-you notes whenever someone does something nice for you, or telephone to express your gratitude.
- Listening more and talking less, especially about yourself.

As you are thinking about grammar and manners, why not make a list of all those things you learned as a young boy or girl from your parents that would be of value and could be shared. I'll bet you have some wonderful examples. Let's share these old-time values.

 This week, concentrate on practicing good manners.

41

To Be Honest with You...

Honest, it's easier to remember the truth.

As children, we learned that the Ten Commandments included "Thou shall not lie." As very young children, we learned from our parents and teachers that lying is wrong. Most people, young and old, agree that honesty is the best policy.

Besides the importance of following God's Commandments, there are many very good reasons for being an honest person, which, of course, means telling the truth. One important reason is that honesty is considered moral, and dishonesty is considered immoral. Honesty is the value of speaking truth and creating trust in the minds of others.

Since honesty helps to form bonds of trust in human relationships, and certainly in close friendships, it is and should be a high priority in most lives. It should be natural and should happen almost always without even thinking about it. There are some situations that do require additional analysis, because we don't want to hurt the feelings of those whom we love. Honesty is the best practice in all situations. Sometimes, however, telling the complete truth would serve no purpose and would cause pain. This is where good judgment is vital.

Honesty generally is considered virtuous behavior and is a positive ingredient in the success of most situations. Honesty simplifies communication in that honest statements can be trusted at face value.

It is much, much easier to speak the truth. It is difficult to remember lies. Many think that "Oh what a tangled web we weave, when first we practice to deceive" was originated by Agatha Christie in her book, *Spider's Web*. Some say the credit for this quotation should be given to Shakespeare, but it actually was first written by Sir Walter Scott. So to you, Sir Walter, thanks for this often-quoted saying that is easy to understand and remember.

Mark Twain said, "If you tell the truth you don't have to remember anything." Abraham Lincoln said, "No man has a good enough memory to make a successful liar."

How often in business, or in everyday dealings with associates and friends, do you hear this said: "To be honest with you" or with even more emphasis, "To be **perfectly** honest with you"? Or perhaps you receive an answer of "Honestly, I don't know" or some other phrase with the words honest, honesty or honestly. Why is it necessary for a person to explain that he or she is being honest—even perfectly honest?

When someone uses this "honesty" gambit to clarify or explain, are they implying that sometimes they don't tell the truth? If that is the case, should the person say, "This may or may not be the truth" and continue with the statement? In so doing, they would be leaving it up to you to decide whether or not it is true. In business, as in personal life, there are the little half-truths or little white lies that make an occasional appearance. These can and should be avoided just by being honest and smart about what is said.

Here are a few examples of common little white lies in the workplace that can be avoided:

- "I was late because I got stuck in traffic." Why not just say you're sorry about being late and will more than make up for it during the week.
- When the boss asks you to do something you say, "That's a great idea and exactly what I was thinking." There is no need to always think the boss has great ideas that are the same as yours. Tell him or her what you had planned and try to use a combination of the two plans.
- "Everything is okay." It's okay to say you could use a little help or encourage discussion about the job to be done.
- There is no need to make up anything. If you don't know the answer, or are unsure, it is always right to say you need to check on it or you simply don't know. It is never right to lie about it.
- "I had to wait for Bill to finish his part before I could finish. That is why the project is late." If this statement is a lie, it is bad. If it is true, it is still bad. It is up to you to compensate for others on the team to make sure the project or job assignment gets finished on time.

Remember, we are not politicians so we have no need to lie. Thomas Jefferson said, "Honesty is the first chapter of the book of wisdom." Wouldn't it be wonderful if we had more politicians who were wise and honest? I know Thomas Jefferson and his many friends had this in mind for our country.

To be **perfectly honest** with you, that is what I believe our country and our politicians need most today—wisdom and honesty.

Give thanks for all the wise and honest friends you have.

42

Who Changed the Subject?

Changing the subject can be worth the challenge.

Almost everyone knows there are two subjects that shouldn't be discussed unless everyone within hearing distance is in complete agreement. And even then, it might be a mistake, because there are those who like to debate and it doesn't matter to them which side they take. The two subjects to avoid are politics and religion. Some say there is a third, sex, but we won't include this today.

So, why do we often get into discussions about politics and religion? There is no possible way that a liberal is going to become a conservative or vice versa during a single discussion—perhaps even during a lifetime—so why try? The same is true of someone who doesn't believe there is a God and life after death, or for a believer to be convinced there is not a God who loves us. Here, as compared to political viewpoints, there might be better reasons to try.

Maybe a reason and a seemingly good one for entering into these discussions is because we care. We want only the best for our friends and family and that may take time, patience and understanding. Even if there are differences of opinion, agreeing to disagree might be an acceptable solution, at least for the short term.

In most cases, it is best to avoid discussion of any subject that might result in ill feelings. Planning ahead not to discuss certain subjects, or changing the subject if a troublesome subject comes up, is a good idea. This will result in a much more enjoyable time together.

There have been a number of occasions when a group of friends have been together and one person, for one reason or another, will suddenly be off on another subject without warning. It becomes confusing, and some good information can easily be lost. So one person in our group suggested that if you are going to change the subject, clap your hands twice to let everyone know a new subject is on the way. Clapping twice rather than once is much more effective in getting everyone's attention. I suggest that if you are going to try this clapping attention-getter to advise that a new subject is on its way, you take the time to explain what you are doing. Just clapping twice without an explanation might make people think you are a little weird.

If you just want to change the subject because it is dragging on too long, is getting boring or is bothering people, here are some tips on how to proceed:

- Take the initiative to switch a conversation when you notice it is getting old, boring or upsetting to any in the group. You can do it.
- It doesn't have to be an abrupt change in the subject, which would be too obvious. It is fairly easy to branch out from the main subject in small steps. For instance, if someone is spending way too much time talking about their recent trip to Spain, you can ask others in the group to tell something about their favorite country.
- The goal in changing the subject should be to move on to a new subject without shifting the center of attention to you or your main interests. Try to bring others into the conversation by talking about their interests or their family.
- Best of all is to be a kind and caring listener, and everyone will think you are a masterful conversationalist and fun to be with.

 Focus on being a kind and caring listener.

43

Balance Likes and Dislikes

Use a scale to evaluate the good, the bad and the salvageable.

If you are unhappy and thinking about changing jobs, it is a good idea, before making any changes, to analyze your present situation. One way to do this is to list the things you like about your job. After listing them, rank the top ten in order of what you feel is the most important. These would be things such as liking the people you work with, reasonable pay and benefits and a clean, modern and safe facility.

Then list things you would like to see changed or improved at your workplace. These could be things like wanting improved communication with your boss or with management. Another example might be wanting better performance reviews so that you would know how to work smarter and be better prepared for advancement.

Both of these exercises have to do with your job or your workplace. If you're not employed, or don't have a workplace, you could use this same thought process for an organization to which you belong, your church or even your personal family environment.

How important to you are the items on the top-ten list of things you like most about your job, organization, church or family situation? Let's look at your list and mark each item with one of the following:

Very Important
Important
Not so important
Not important

Likewise, look at the list of things you would like to see changed or improved. Add the same notations to this list. Are there any on this list that are, realistically speaking, very important?

How do these two lists compare? Is your list of likes positive, and do you feel good about them? How really important are the items on the list of things you would like to see changed? Could you be happy and live with things the way they are if some minor changes were made? Or, do you feel that unless some things change dramatically, you're out of there?

What we are trying to do here is make a job comparison of likes and dislikes. Think of a balance scale with all your likes on one side of the scale and all your dislikes (things you would like to see changed) on the other side. Which way does the scale tip and by how much?

You know the scale can be moved, mentally, one way or the other, based on who is loading the likes and dislikes. When loading the scale, is it with an optimistic, or pessimistic, frame of mind? Optimists will look for the bright side of life and for the positive aspects of the job most of the time, while pessimists will be thinking about the job in a negative or critical way much of the time. This not only shows up on the scale, it shows up often in real-life situations.

Have you also wondered why so many people seem to enjoy complaining about their boss, their company or both? Think about how often you are drawn into a negative conversation about what is happening or not happening at work. You know this is a total waste of time and energy and it saps the creative juices right out of an organization.

Doing this rather basic analysis of likes and dislikes helps to put the overall situation more in the right perspective. Be honest with yourself when answering whether your job-scale balance presently is in the right or wrong direction. If it's pointing upward, with important positives, that's great. Work to make it even more positive. If, however, it's pointing downward, with negatives, determine what can be done to change the balance of your job or your company.

Let's "accentuate the positive, eliminate the negative, latch on to the affirmative, and don't mess with Mister In-Between."

The next time you hear someone say something critical about your company or any of the employees, tell that person the top two or three things you like most about the company. Ask them what they like most.

44

CULTIVATE CHARACTER

No Dog in the Fight

Before acting, stop to think whether or not your interests
are at stake.

Isn't it amazing how often we find ourselves getting involved in situations in which we really have no right to be?

What is it that makes this happen? Is it curiosity, even knowing that "curiosity killed the cat," and that they have nine lives and we but one? Or is it that we feel we can contribute something worthwhile that surely must be needed or appreciated? Would this be an ego thing? Maybe it's just a strong desire to be a part of whatever is happening, good or bad. If it is good, then that is positive; if it is bad, we should be able to turn it into something good and positive. Makes sense doesn't it—or does it?

Could it be that our help is not always needed or wanted? Maybe that is also true about our advice. Is it necessary for someone to have to ask for help or ask for advice? Or, in today's world, is it okay to just jump right in and let them know what needs to be done or needs to be done differently?

Not too long ago, I heard a friend talking to his wife as she was complaining about how certain trees were being trimmed at the lake. She felt the trees were not being trimmed correctly. Even though these were not her trees, she felt she should do something about it. I think she understood what was happening when her husband said to her, "Dear, you don't have a dog in this fight." I hadn't heard the expression before, but it certainly is easy to understand and clearly puts things in perspective.

I really do like this message and so does my wife. It is amazing how many times we have used this "You or we don't have a dog in this fight." It is a wake-up call to back off or to just stay out of it. If we have used this expression so often since we first heard it, I wonder how many times in the past we got into a dog fight without owning a dog. Probably quite a few.

We were at Sam's Club the other day and some guy who was trying to steal a TV set was caught. There were three Sam's Club employees holding the thief, waiting for the police to arrive. I felt I should go over to offer help in case they needed it. I almost did so until my dear wife reminded me that I didn't have a dog in that fight. I didn't have a dog in the fight and I didn't even know if the dog in the fight was armed. So, what was I thinking? Perhaps it was remembering the saying, "It's not the size of the dog in the fight, it's the fight in the dog that counts." How this would help in this case I really don't know.

Did you know that President George Bush and Secretary of State James Baker used "I don't have a dog in that fight" in the 1980s and 1990s? For them, it meant, "I don't have an interest in this matter." It is not known where or when the saying originated. I don't think it was at Possum Kingdom Lake for them, but it was for me.

To get involved or not to get involved, aye, that's the question. Before answering, consider whether or not you have a dog in the fight. It works.

Don't get into a dog fight if your dog isn't there or if you don't have a dog.

45

COACHING

What Is Mentoring?

A mentor is a cheerleader.

Have you had a mentor at some time in your life? Do you have one now or are you a mentor to anyone else? Take a little time and think about the mentors you have had and what an influence they had on your life, if any.

Let's take a look at mentoring.

Origin of the term mentor or mentoring

We cannot be sure of the true origin of the word; several stories present different versions. A few examples follow:

1. In Homer's *The Odyssey,* Mentor is a trusted friend to whom Ulysses leaves the care of his household when he departs for the Trojan War. Athena, disguised as Mentor, guides Odysseus's son, Telemachus, in his search for his father.

2. In 1698, François Fénelon was appointed by King Louis XIV as a tutor to the king's grandson, the Duke of Burgundy. Fénelon, in his book, *Les Adventures de Télémaque,* uses the term "sage counselor" to describe his main character, the goddess Minerva who appears as Mentor. The book is clearly an imitation of Homer's *The Odyssey,* and the lessons expounded by Mentor in the book are both more educational than those of Homer's Mentor and are directed toward guiding his pupil in how to become a peaceful and wise monarch. This more closely fits the description of what a mentor should be; thus, many favor this Mentor over Homer's Mentor as the original.

3. La Grotte de Niaux is a prehistoric cave located high in the Pyrenees in southern France. The cave has paintings estimated to have been created somewhere between 12,000 and 9,000 BC. There are numerous paintings showing a group of men taking children to what at that time was considered the edge or end of their physical world.

Some believe that the origin of the term mentor comes from what has been translated in these ancient depictions as men taking children on a tour.

It probably doesn't matter which origin you choose. You can be more traditional and choose Homer's; more intellectual and choose Fénelon's; or more creative and imaginative and choose "men on a tour." Personally, I like all three.

What is a mentor?

There are many definitions of the word mentor. One is that a mentor is a wise and trusted counselor or teacher. Another says that a mentor is a consistent friend and role model. Robert Lewis, in *The Quest for the Authentic Manhood,* has five comments about a mentor:

- A mentor is one who supports rather than competes with you.
- A mentor is one who is primarily a cheerleader, not a critic.
- A mentor is one who seeks to encourage the development of your gifts while seeking to protect you from costly mistakes.
- A mentor is one who admires and delights in you because he instinctively recognizes your value and untapped potential.
- A mentor is not necessarily a close friend, but he is a close confidant.

Another fine description of a mentor is that of being a tour guide. I think this is very good because having a tour guide can be of such value when you are traveling or venturing into unknown territories. So wouldn't it be of even greater value to have an everyday tour guide or mentor to guide you through life? In this case, the mentor is the tour guide. Perhaps there is a connection here with being a "tour guide" and "men on a tour."

Mentoring generally has been associated with business. Up and coming younger managers had mentors to guide them along in their career development and their climb up the corporate ladder.

The success of mentoring in business has led to the expansion of mentoring in schools, organizations and in personal life. Partners in Education (PIE) had over 1,100 mentors in elementary through high school in Wichita Falls, Texas. This is an impressive number, as it should be, because PIE is an impressive organization with great leadership.

Think back to mentors you have had and how they contributed to the real you. Give them a call or write them a letter.

46

End of an Era

It doesn't have to happen for what is important.

For many years, a group of guys from Wichita Falls traveled to Creede, Colorado, in September to fish for trout. The location was Streams Lake, which was a beautiful place in the mountains with a scenic lake, flowing streams and meadow. Usually, the fishing was very good.

There was an old and rather primitive cabin with two bedrooms and a sleeping dorm, which was affectionately referred to as the dormitory. Those who slept in the dormitory were members of a special fraternity called the "dormitory." Getting a good night's sleep in this noisy dormitory was almost impossible, but that didn't really seem to matter.

The cabin didn't have running water and the facilities were two outhouses about 30 yards to the side of the cabin. There was a long, rough, bumpy dirt road that led to the cabin. A four-wheel-drive vehicle was necessary to climb the long road. So, what made this location so special? Why did everyone look forward to being invited again to go to Streams Lake?

Was it the fishing? Was it the companionship? Was it the evenings around the campfire after a long day of fishing? Was it the atmosphere of an old rustic cabin? Was it the food? Was it the stories in the dormitory? Was it being with good friends? Was it having someone else clean your fish? Was it having fly fishing instructions from one of the experts? Was it hiking to the upper meadows and to the water falls? Was it Doc Anderson's hospitality? The answer is YES. It was all those things and more.

One year, the ranch was sold and we could no longer go to Streams Lake. What is sad is that we never found a replacement for it, and we stopped going on our September fishing trips. We gave up something very special. We had a reunion a few years ago, but it wasn't the same. This was the end of an era.

For over 20 years, a group of guys has met for lunch in the back room of the Piccadilly Cafeteria every Thursday. A number of them were also part of the Streams Lake group. Two of both the lunch group and the fishing group and four from the fishing group are no longer with us. We thought about them today as we come to the end of another era. The end of the era is the closing of the Piccadilly Cafeteria. Our two comrades from both groups are Bob Jones and Travis Regan. Four other fishing buddies are Jim Lonergan, Ralph Morgan, Dick Harris and Lane West. We miss them a great deal. We miss our time together in Colorado. We miss them at the Piccadilly. It is the end of another era.

We are not going to make the same mistake with this end of an era that we made with the fishing era. We are going to start a new one by continuing the meetings at a new location. What was most important about what we had as the era came to an end was not the food, not the location, not the back room, not the friendly, helpful employees of the Piccadilly Cafeteria; it was the enjoyment and value of being together with friends. It was the sharing of stories, of jokes, of experiences. That is what is important and it is up to us to keep it going—and we will.

This is the message in this *Actions Speak Louder* action. The end of an era doesn't have to be the end of what is really important. What is important can be continued in the new era if we want it to be. It is up to us to make it happen. Consider whether you had an era that recently ended that could be started again as the beginning of a new era. Maybe you can make it happen.

 Move forward from the end of an era into the beginning of a new one with optimism and enthusiasm.

47

Smiling Is Infectious

Smile and the whole world smiles with you.

Most of us want to make a difference in the lives of others. I believe there is a very natural drive and motivation to make a difference, to contribute, to make this a better world. Some just don't know how to make it happen.

Recently, I was asked: "How do you get started in making a difference?" The answer really has to do with what is right for the person asking the question.

Many probably are making much more of a difference in the lives of others than they realize. So, the question might be how to do more, or something different, in addition to what is already being done that is rewarding and is making a difference.

One suggestion would be to start with little things that can be done every day that will become routine and natural. The goal is to do those things that will be appreciated and that will result in increased happiness for both the giver and the receiver.

One thought is to smile more often and to share your smile with more people. "Frown and you frown alone," it is sometimes said, "but smile and the whole world smiles with you." Maybe the whole world is a bit of a stretch, but smiles can be powerful and definitely contagious.

What is so powerful about smiles and why are they contagious? Smiles are powerful because we are naturally drawn to people who smile; there is some kind of attraction to them. It seems that we want to know a smiling person and want to avoid a frowning one. Frowns push people away, while smiles bring people together and make them feel good.

Smiles are contagious, because when someone is smiling they brighten up the environment, and this makes others want to smile and be happy. Smiles are contagious, something good to catch and even better to pass on to others. Smiles are a good thing to be infected with, not something you take shots to avoid.

An unknown author wrote this poem:

Smiling is infectious,
You can catch it like the flu.
Someone smiled at me today
And I started smiling too.

Some people have a very natural smile and they always look good in pictures. Others have a hard time smiling for pictures and seem to always look silly or too serious. I am the latter and my wife is the former. I think in everyday life it is easier to smile than to pose for pictures with a natural smile.

Even so, sometimes we just don't feel like smiling, or it isn't coming naturally, and we are in a situation in which smiling would be the right thing to do. What do we do? One suggestion is to think happy thoughts. Probably the easiest way to a great smile is to be happy. Another way is to think of something amusing or a funny joke you recently heard.

You know you can get sad and even cry thinking about certain movies or books. *Field of Dreams* does that to me. It can be the same way with happy movies, books or thoughts that result in natural smiles. Try this sometime.

Consider smiling a wonderful way to make a difference in others' lives. Think about these thoughts from another unknown author:

A smile costs nothing but gives much. It enriches those who receive without making poorer those who give. It takes but a moment, but the memory of it sometimes lasts forever. None is so rich or mighty that he can get along without it and none is so poor that he cannot be made rich by it. Yet a smile cannot be bought, begged, borrowed, or stolen, for it is something that is of no value to anyone until it is given away. Some people are too tired to give you a smile. Give them one of yours, as none needs a smile so much as he who has no more to give.

Make a difference in others' lives by practicing little acts of kindness. Start by smiling often.

48

Thanks, Coach

I never played the game.

There is only a handful of Division I football coaches who didn't play the game in college. Charlie Weis, the current head football coach at Notre Dame, is one. A past season leads many to think that Notre Dame made a mistake in hiring Charlie away from the New England Patriots to be their answer to a return to national prominence. For some time it wasn't working. Can a coach really be effective and relate to the ballplayers if he hasn't walked in their shoes with cleats?

Howard Cosell, a popular and controversial sports newscaster on Monday Night Football, had never played the game. In fact, he wrote an interesting book titled, *I never played the game.* As I remember it, there were two main messages in his book about never having played the game. One was actually about playing football, and the other was about following what others told him to do—meaning to "play their game."

Some liked Howard and some didn't, but there were two things that everyone had to agree on about him. He was colorful and he did love the game of football. He added excitement to even boring Monday night games.

I thought Lou Holtz was another coach who had never played the game. But that's not true; he did play football at Kent State University. I guess I just pictured him as not having played football because of his size.

Lou Holtz is a former NCAA football and NFL head coach and a talented author, television commentator and motivational speaker. Holtz is the only coach in NCAA history to lead six different programs to bowl games and the only coach to guide four different programs to final top-20 rankings.

Lou Holtz, like many other successful college football coaches, shows how important it is to have a leader with the right priorities in life, knowledge of the game, experience, understanding and appreciation for the players and a love of the game. He is a fine example of being disciplined and yet highly motivational. He truly is a master at what he does.

All who have participated in athletics can recall memories, probably good coaches you have had. I think we remember more the good coaches who kne were doing and really cared about the kids. They seemed to know who the ri to put in each position, and how best to help each player reach his or her po

The successful coaches also knew about the competition—what defense t offense to run. I don't recall coaches who didn't play the game in their yout didn't love the game, no matter which game it was. Coaches live a very reward are much appreciated by so many of their athletes and their families. The prol I don't think we expressed our appreciation of them as much as we should h

If we were in the position to select a coach for our football team, we would w these most important characteristics:

- Has played the game
- Loves the game
- Has experience and knowledge of the game
- Knows how to motivate the players
- Demonstrated prior success with players and has a winning attitude
- Has the right priorities in life

Football is a lot like war in many ways. There is strategy. There is comm winning. There is support of the players or troops that is critical. There is kno the competition (enemy) that is absolutely necessary. There is the need to recog offense is needed and when defense is needed. There is the need to have equipment possible and be the best trained. When to let the coach coach and w the coach call the plays to win are essential to achieving victory.

If you were able to choose a Commander in Chief, wouldn't you also want som has knowledge of the military, love of our troops, experience in the military, kno motivate our troops and can convey a winning attitude that is consistent over th

Wouldn't it be a disaster to have someone who doesn't meet any of these cr our Commander in Chief? It could happen if we become complacent and let who hasn't played the game choose our coach.

Contact a coach from the past or his o family and let them know how much th were appreciated.

I'm Sorry

good apology has three parts.

How important is it to say I'm sorry and make it sound as though you mean it? When nking about this, consider a range of happenings, from little things that deserve some d of apology to serious situations that could mean the loss of a friendship, serious pression, or even loss of a job. Both kinds of situations should merit some kind of action your part.

Examples of little things could be forgetting a birthday; not including someone, who bably should have been invited, in an event; or forgetting to go to someone's party. A one might be spreading mean, and perhaps untrue, gossip about an individual— mething that causes hurt and anger. Afterwards, you might think, "Why in the world I I ever say that? I wish I could take it back." Small or large mistakes like these do need apology.

I have been thinking about this lately, because during almost all elections these days, e politicians and the media are saying so much that is questionable. So often things are d that are not true, or the real meaning is not received as it was intended. Then the litician or news reporter is criticized either for not making an apology or for making one at doesn't sound sincere. Even if the apology is given in a sincere way, oftentimes, nditions or excuses are associated with it. So, it is not a real apology.

There is a very moving and inspirational story about a professor at Carnegie Mellon niversity. His name is Randy Pausch. He has become well known because of his "Last cture," which he gave a few years ago. You see, Randy, a young man in his 40s with ree small children, learned that he had cancer and had just three to six months to live. his motivated Randy to give his last lecture to his students. The lecture was not about ath, but about life. I recommend you search this on the Internet or use the link below see and listen to his lecture.

I would like to share a few thoughts from Randy's lecture that hit home to me when thinking about saying "I'm sorry." Randy told about some guiding principles in his life that helped him succeed. One was to always tell the truth. Another was to apologize when you have done something wrong. He said a good apology has three important parts:

1. Saying—I'm sorry
2. Saying—It's my fault
3. Saying—How do I make it right?

You know the saying, "Any job worth doing is worth doing well." This makes sense, doesn't it? Well, I would say that any apology worth doing is worth doing well. An insincere or bad apology could make the situation even worse, so if you are going to do it, do it in the right way. Making an apology in the right way requires thoughtful consideration, planning, empathy and good timing.

Listen to Randy Pausch's "Last Lecture" at:
http://video.stumbleupon.com/
?s=ithct48cqw&i=ufcchmyxqsuj9vwsemax

Five Golden Rings

It's time to sing along.

December is when we seem to listen to music much more than any other time of the year. Christmas music is playing everywhere and it's wonderful. Music is playing in the stores and on the radio as it always does, but I don't think we listen to it in the same way as we do during the days before Christmas.

Christmas music plays to our emotions, sometimes making us feel good and sometimes sad. Many times it makes us think of past holidays, and sometimes it makes us think about the real reason for celebrating Christmas.

Our local symphony orchestra presented "A Family-Style Christmas" this December, with a full evening of music by the orchestra and choral groups. The local university singers sang "Still, Still, Still" and "The Little Drummer Boy." These are two of my favorite Christmas songs, so I was very happy to see them on the program. These are the kinds of songs that have the melody and words to truly move you and make you want to sing along—words that have to do with Christmas:

> *Sleep, sleep, sleep,*
> *'Tis the eve of our Savior's birth*

And

> *Come they told me, pa rum pum pum pum*
> *A new born king to see, pa rum pum, pum, pum*

Then there are many songs that are sung at Christmastime that have really nothing to do with the birth of Jesus. Examples of these kinds of songs are "Rudolf the Red

Nosed Reindeer," "Jingle Bells," "Frosty the Snowman," "Santa Clause is Coming to Town" and many others.

The symphony orchestra and the combined choirs presented "The Twelve Days of Christmas." This song is usually seen as one of those songs like "Jingle Bells" and others meant to be delightful but nonsensical songs for children to enjoy. Some say there is much more to this song than the lyrics seem to say. Others say, no, it is what it is, nothing more. It is up to you to decide how you want to enjoy the song. I say, why not in both ways?

Actually, the twelve days of Christmas are the twelve days starting on Christmas day and going to the beginning of Epiphany. But so be it. It is okay to think of the twelve days of Christmas leading up to Christmas day. It has been suggested that it is a song of Christian instruction from the 16th century religious wars in England, with hidden references to the basic teachings of the faith.

What is being said in "The Twelve Days of Christmas" is that my "true love" mentioned in the song is God. "Me," who receives the presents, is all persons of the Christian faith. Each day represents some aspect of the Christian faith that was important for children to learn. This is what the days represent:

On the 1st day of Christmas my "true love" (God) gave to "me" (Christians) A Partridge (Jesus Christ) in a Pear Tree.

2nd day—Two Turtle Doves—the Old and New Testaments

3rd day—Three French Hens—the three theological virtues: faith, hope and love

4th day—Four Calling Birds—the four Gospels: Mathew, Mark, Luke and John

5th day—Five Golden Rings—the five books of the Old Testament known as the Torah

6th day—Six Geese A-laying—the six days of creation

7th day—Seven Swans A-swimming—the seven gifts of the Holy Spirit: prophecy, ministry, teaching, exhortation, giving, leading and compassion

8th day—Eight Maids A-milking—the Eight Beatitudes

9th day—Nine Ladies Dancing—the nine fruits of the Holy Spirit: love, joy, peace, patience, kindness, generosity, faithfulness, gentleness and self-control

10th day—Ten Lords A-leaping—the Ten Commandments

11th day—Eleven Pipers Piping—the eleven faithful Apostles (Judas is not included)

12th day—Twelve Drummers Drumming—the twelve points of doctrine in the Apostles' Creed

How can you not want to join the singing when the chorus comes to the Five Golden Rings? Whether this is just five golden rings or refers to the five books of the Old Testament, you still want to sing "Five Golden Rings," don't you?

If, today, you hear this famous and popular song during the Christmas season, what's wrong with thinking about these Christian references, whether their origin was factual in the 16th century or not? I think it is timely today in the 21st century.

Spend quality time singing your favorite Christmas songs with family and friends this holiday season.

51

Contract for Life

Write a personal contract with yourself.

You will hate this action. Yes, it's true, but if just one person is motivated to enter into a contract for life, this action will be worth reading and sharing.

What is a contract for life? It is a written, personal contract that you make with yourself, committing to making those lifestyle changes that will increase the opportunities for greater happiness and improved health in your life.

When we buy a house, set up a will or living trust, or generally make major commitments that have financial consequences, we give them a great deal of thought and analysis. We do this to make sure what we are doing is what we want to do.

Then the process usually includes the involvement of professionals who charge us to make sure we are doing it the right way. This includes signing contracts or formal documents that protect us and prove to anyone involved that this is what we want and what we intend to do. Generally, these are binding until we legally change them or complete the contract.

This is an accepted way of handling such events in our lives. You could buy or sell your own home and handle the financing or write your own will. Maybe it would work, and maybe it wouldn't. Doing it yourself presents some very real risks, and in the long run, you might end up spending more money to get what you really want. So, isn't it worth doing it right in the first place?

The same is true concerning our lives. We should all know what is best for us to ensure a happier and healthier life. When we grow older, we want to feel good and we want to be able to do those things that are important to us. This means for many of us that we should be doing certain things differently now.

There are many areas in which this is so, but these are three examples to consider:

- Stop smoking
- Lose weight—attain your healthy weight
- Relationship with God

You might want to add other personal challenges.

If you are a smoker or are significantly overweight, you have a choice. You can decide to do nothing if you enjoy smoking or eating so much that you are willing to give up years, health and energy. It is your decision to make. Procrastination is not an answer.

Are smoking and eating higher priorities to you than life itself? You might think you can live with, or accept, being overweight or continuing smoking. This means you are willing to accept the consequences of this decision. You cannot live with your present situation and not know what you might be giving up in your life.

Consider priorities: Isn't giving up something that is not so important to gain something very important, meaning your life, worth doing?

The third area, which is undoubtedly the most important of all, is knowing that you are right with God. This more than anything else has to do with life. I am not going to say more about this, but I felt an action encouraging readers to make significant lifestyle changes, to have a contract for life and to use professional help would not be complete without including God. Your minister could be your professional help.

Take the time to write a personal contract with yourself to make the right lifestyle changes. Whether it is to stop smoking, lose a certain amount of weight, get in better shape, or strengthen your religious beliefs, consider using a professional to help you succeed. Few can do it alone.

Many can succeed with help, so why not commit to a serious contract between yourself and your professional? You have many choices for professional help, but your doctor might be the first one to include in your contract.

Write your contract in specific terms with goals for success. In buying a house, would you write a contract that doesn't give you ownership of the house? Would you write a will that doesn't give your estate to your family as you intend? No, of course not. Then you, likewise, wouldn't write a contract for life that doesn't provide the necessary actions for increased opportunity for long-term health and happiness. Write a contract that gives you what you really want—your life. Following your contract for life will require dedication and determination. You can do it.

Decide to make this a very special year for you and your family.

52

Personal Calendar for a Special Year

This is the year to...

Have you ever thought about making your own calendar for a full year? Not just one in which you write down birthdays and anniversaries, but one in which you plan things you want to do or accomplish during the year. This would be a personal calendar in which each month is a special month for doing something. Think about doing this for this year or the next twelve months. Try using this example to get started:

January: Develop plans, set goals and make fun resolutions for the year. Review what happened last year. What should be repeated and what should be changed? Keep the good memories in mind and visible.

February: This month should be Valentine's month. Do valentine things for your sweetheart. Practice little acts of kindness. This could very likely turn into a good habit that lasts all year long, and then, why not the following year? And then, the following year?

March: Begin at least one physical outdoor activity such as golf, hiking, tennis or biking. If you are a golfer, it wouldn't hurt to start practicing this month. You know a drive is one stroke and so is a putt. Doesn't seem right does it? Where should you spend time practicing?

April: Start a garden by planting beautiful flowers. Pay your taxes. Oh, what fun we can have in April. Flowers have wonderful smells and taxes stink.

May: Deliver May baskets and remember how important it is to smell the roses. Take time to enjoy and share your blessings.

June: Celebrate graduations, weddings and other occasions. Look for these opportunities. Send notes and gifts when they are not expected.

July: Take some interesting local weekend or day trips. Consider educational and historical experiences as well as those that are just for fun. Keep a log or scrapbook and share the good times with friends.

August: Go on a real vacation of one to two weeks, traveling to a new place or places that you haven't visited before. Have at least one highlight of the day each day during the trip.

September: Arrange for old friends to join you for a high-school or college mini-reunion.

October: Work on a favorite indoor hobby or project. Organize something that needs organizing. Doesn't sound like much fun, but the results will be rewarding.

November: Make the month a time for giving thanks, including all the good times and accomplishments of the first ten months of the year.

December: Celebrate the birth of Jesus Christ. Help someone or some family who needs help. Take advantage of the many Christmas activities.

There will be many other events each month, and there will be busy schedules with conflicts, for sure. Maybe this calendar is a good way to help ensure that you and your family do the things that are most important to you. Have your very own personal calendar.

Plan to do those things this year that are most important to you.

53

Little Acts Make a Big Difference

Communicate with love in mind.

Several actions were about making a difference in your life and the lives of others. There were suggestions about getting started with little acts of kindness and thoughts on making a difference in the community.

These are good thoughts, but so would be suggestions about making a difference at home. Sometimes we tend to take things most dear to us for granted. We forget to do those things that make a difference for our spouses or our family members. I think some of the reasons for this are because we get busy, have pressures at work and experience numerous demands on our time. This is life, isn't it?

Thinking about making a difference with our spouses led to I Corinthians:

> *Love is patient; love is kind; love is not envious or boastful or arrogant or rude. It does not insist on its own way; it is not irritable or resentful; it does not rejoice in wrongdoing, but rejoices in the truth. It bears all things, believes all things, hopes all things, endures all things.*
> I Corinthians 13: 4-8
>
> *And now faith, hope, and love abide, these three; and the greatest of these is love.*
> I Corinthians 13: 13

Isn't it amazing that this was written about 2,000 years ago, is so profound and continues today to be so timely? We can look at each of these love traits, do a self-evaluation and decide where we want to make changes—changes that will make a difference.

Are we as patient and kind as we should be? Are we sometimes irritable or resentful when we shouldn't be? Are we as supportive and understanding of our spouse as we should be? Do we oftentimes insist on our own way? Do we sometimes speak too quickly and say something that is arrogant or rude? These are questions we should ask ourselves if we do truly want to make a difference at home.

Practicing these love traits requires a relationship in which both parties have a strong foundation of commitment, communication and compromise. In the center of commitment and compromise is communication, because without good and open communication, commitment won't last very long and compromise will be almost impossible. So, the focus should be on communication.

Here are a few tips on communication with love in mind:

- It is almost as important to think about what you shouldn't say as about what you should say. Not everything needs to be said; some things are best kept private and quiet.
- Speak only when you are sure you have only positive and loving things to say. If you are upset or mad, wait until another time for your communication. Timing is so important and saying the wrong thing can be so hurtful. Just don't risk it.
- Don't ask the question if you are not prepared for the answer.
- Don't answer the question if the one asking the question is not prepared for the answer. Not all questions require an answer.
- Think about what you have said. Is there any possibility that what you said might not be understood and the wrong message might be given? If there is any doubt at all, go the extra mile for loving communication.

Make a difference in your spouse's or family's life and you will be making a difference in your life too.

Truth or Consequences

It's all about trust.

Top management and owners of businesses ask themselves questions about who they are, where they are going and how they are going to get there. These are important questions to ask on a regular basis, and especially when critical decisions are to be made concerning the future of the company.

There are three questions that I believe should be answered first in order for management to lead the company in the right way. Answers to these questions are necessary to ensure that decisions are made and actions are taken that support the guiding vision of the company. They are the following:

1. Is it more important to have great customers, or to have great employees?
2. Should the company's number-one focus be on customers, employees or the shareholders?
3. What is the company's most important asset—customers, employees, products, distribution, name recognition or what?

After answering these questions, there are some logical follow-up questions that probably should be asked concerning the present situation at the company. If management says the answer to all three questions is employees, the question would be whether they are acting as though employees were actually most important to them. Do they need to make changes?

I firmly believe that it is most important to have great employees. The number-one focus should be on employees; they are the company's most important asset. The success of ABB was the result of having outstanding customer focus, but it took really great employees to make this happen. Thus, it is both, but great employees are the ones who develop great customers.

This would mean that attracting and retaining great employees should be the most important focus for the companies that answered these questions with employees at the top.

We could compile a list of important characteristics of great employees to help with the analysis of the present situation. The list might include some of the following:

- Good communication skills, including listening
- Analytical and problem-solving skills
- Leadership skills
- Interpersonal abilities
- Team player
- Dependable
- Loyal
- Positive attitude
- Self-motivated
- Flexible
- Competent
- Committed
- Hard-working
- Ethical
- Honest and trustworthy

Do great employees have to excel in all these areas or have all these characteristics? No, they don't, but there is one that is an absolute must and that is "honest and trustworthy." How can management make the right decisions if they don't trust or believe every employee? An employee cannot be great if he or she cannot be trusted and does not tell the truth all the time. They should find work elsewhere.

We say this about great employees, but do we say the same thing about politicians or great politicians? How many great politicians are there today?

Unfortunately, we saw candidates (just a few) for the presidency of the United States who were not honest and couldn't be trusted. It seems easy for some of them simply not to tell the truth. I think some of these politicians don't tell the truth because they do not have strong basic core convictions and principles. They must believe the end justifies the means.

In business it is absolutely necessary to have employees and leaders who can be trusted and are honest people who tell the truth. What about in politics? Isn't it even more important that the leaders of our country be people who can be trusted and who can be counted on to tell the truth? If not, shouldn't they also find work elsewhere?

Focus on being a great employee, a great friend and a great family member.

55

CULTIVATE CHARACTER

Your Own GPS

Priorities determine directions.

We have a GPS installed in our van. We love it. It has helped us so many times as we traveled to see our grandkids perform and participate in various activities and sports. It is easy to use, and we even get a kick out of the instructions the gal in the sky gives us. How does she know?

She always wants to send us on the interstate, and sometimes we have a better way to go. After a number of "make a u-turn whenever possible" instructions are not followed, she adjusts to what we are doing, and I guess she learns to live with it. We joke about it, because she probably is not very happy with our not following her instructions. After all, she has a much better view of everything from up there in the sky than we do from down here on the ground.

What she doesn't know is that we have traveled this route before and know that at this time of day, it is better to go a different way. It isn't that she is wrong; it is just that some choices should be left up to us. We have the right to override her instructions if we so choose. However, if we are lost or don't really know where we are going, we do rely on her expertise with full confidence that she will get us to the right destination. She even tells us how many miles we have to go and when we will arrive.

Wouldn't it be wonderful if we had a personal GPS system to guide us through life? If we could just program the GPS with our final destination, or perhaps a number of destinations, for different stages during our life, wouldn't that be great? You would think it would help to keep us moving forward in the right direction with the right stops along the way.

Would you like someone in the sky to be watching over you all the time? Would you want to be told when you need to make a U-turn or to change directions when you appear to be off track?

We all know that we have taken different roads in life that haven't always led us to the right destination in the most direct way and in the shortest time. But how serious is this if we somehow do make the adjustments necessary and end up where we want to be?

I think that having a personal GPS would present some problems for us. First of all, we would have to learn how to tell the GPS where we want to go. This would be especially difficult to do if we don't know where we are going or really don't even seem to care about it. And how will we be able to tell our GPS when we want to get there if we haven't determined which detours and stops we want to make along the way? A GPS system isn't designed for drifting without a plan or a destination.

When a personal GPS device is developed and introduced to the market, it will probably come with a lifetime warranty that will require filling out the warranty registration card. The warranty card will require all the basic information you are used to including, if you have ever filled one out, and something more. This something more will require you to list your priorities in life in an order of importance.

By listing your priorities, the Guide in the sky will be able to tell you when you are traveling in a direction contrary to your priorities. You know your priorities and so does He. You also really know when you are taking the wrong path, but you need to be reminded at times. That is why you need your own personal GPS. You probably already have your own GPS system waiting for you to fill out the warranty registration card. Remember, it comes with a life-time warranty.

 Make plans for the rest of the year with your priorities in mind.

56

To Thine Own Self Be True

Who are you and why are you here?

Who are you and why are you here? Interesting questions, aren't they?

Some years ago, an ABB business associate and friend, Pat, and I were visiting one of our ABB supply companies in Heidelberg, Germany. I had been there before, but this was Pat's first visit. Right at the very beginning of the meeting, the managing director looked directly at Pat and asked, "Who are you and why are you here?" It was an interesting and different way to start a meeting, but when you think about it, an efficient way to get to the real purpose of the meeting.

We have kidded about this "Who are you and why are you here?" question many times, and you know, it is often so appropriate.

John Muir, when he was senior minister at the First Christian Church, preached a sermon using an old Indian story to tell about who we really are and why we are here.

"The Little Boy and the Rattlesnake"

The little boy was walking down a path and he came across a rattlesnake. The rattlesnake was getting old. He asked, "Please little boy, can you take me to the top of the mountain? I hope to see the sunset one last time before I die." The little boy answered, "No, Mr. Rattlesnake. If I pick you up, you'll bite me and I'll die." The rattlesnake said, "No, I promise I won't bite you. Just please take me up to the mountain." The little boy thought about it and finally picked up that rattlesnake and took it close to his chest and carried it up to the top of the mountain.

They sat there and watched the sunset together. It was so beautiful. Then after sunset, the rattlesnake turned to the little boy and asked, "Can I go home now? I am tired, and I am old."

The little boy picked up the rattlesnake and again took it to his chest and held it tightly and safely. He came all the way down the mountain holding the snake carefully and took it to his home to give him some food and a place to sleep.

The next day, the rattlesnake turned to the boy and asked, "Please, little boy, will you take me back to my home now? It is time for me to leave this world, and I would like to be at my home now." The little boy felt he had been safe all this time and the snake had kept his word, so he would take it home as asked.

He carefully picked up the snake, took it close to his chest, and carried him back to the woods to its home to die. Just before he laid the rattlesnake down, the rattlesnake turned and bit him in the chest. The little boy cried out and threw the snake upon the ground. "Mr. Snake, why did you do that? Now I will surely die." The rattlesnake looked up at him and grinned, "You knew what I was when you picked me up."

Is a rattlesnake always a rattlesnake? Can the leopard change its spots? Is a politician always a politician? Is a liberal politician always a liberal politician? Is a conservative politician always a conservative politician?

Some politicians who were running for the office of President of the United States acted like rattlesnakes in many ways, especially telling voters what they thought they wanted to hear.

We should be able to ask each one, "Who are you and why are you here?" And we should expect to receive honest answers, but you know we won't, because "You knew I was a rattlesnake when you picked me up."

So, the lesson to be learned from this little Indian boy is not to believe rattlesnakes when they tell you they won't bite you. You know what rattlesnakes do. They bite you. Likewise with some politicians, they tell you they won't bite you, but when they are in office they become who they are, and you are the one who gets bitten.

How important is it now to ask, "Who is this candidate and why is he here?"

William Shakespeare said, "This above all, to thine own self be true, And it must follow, as the night the day, Thou canst be false to any man."

In the future, we should look for the man or woman who will "be true to thine own self" and can answer honestly the question, "Who are you and why are you here?"

Write your favorite candidates in the next election and ask them, "Who are you and why are you here?"

57

COACHING

It's All about Time

Time management touches every part of our lives.

Does it seem that you never have enough time to do all you want to do? Does it seem that time is going by faster each year? Is it also a question of feeling as though too much time is being spent at work or on the job and maybe too little with the family? Or not enough private time for fun and doing the things you really enjoy?

All of this probably is true for most of us and probably for most of the time. This, then, brings up the question of whether to do anything about the situation. Do we want to live with our present structure and lifestyle, or should we consider making changes?

If the above hits home for you, why not take time to do a little exercise today? If you are so inclined or motivated, please follow along with thinking about and answering the questions below. Even if you are not that motivated, why not just participate for the fun of it and see what happens? You might be surprised:

- How am I actually spending my time? Break time spent into major time categories and have a written document showing how you are spending your time. Know where you are starting in your analysis.
- What are my priorities in life? Know or list your top priorities—probably five top major priorities and another five to ten sub-priorities or actions. For instance, family is probably one of the top five priorities, and sub-priorities or actions could be family related, such as paying for college, taking family vacations, etc.
- Compare your priorities with how you are actually spending your time. What percentage of your time is being spent on your top priorities?
- How much time do I want to free up each week to spend on my top priorities?
- Do you really want to make changes in your lifestyle, structure and allocation of time? Are you serious about doing this or is it just a fleeting thought and exercise?

Assuming the answers to these last questions are yes, you are serious, then further analysis is needed. Let's look at your job:

Suggestions for too much time spent on the job, including work at home:

1. What can I do to become more productive? Where am I wasting time? Be creative in your analysis, considering new technologies, communication tools, improved systems and outside help. Certainly there are some possibilities for improvement.
2. Am I doing other people's work? What can I delegate to others? What do I have to do and what can others do? Do I have to receive and answer all the e-mails that come to me?
3. Can I reduce the amount of time in meetings? What can I do to make the meetings more efficient? Can my company start a policy, or enforce an existing one, of making sure meetings start on time and end on time?
4. Can I take a time-management course, or better, use what I already know? Am I doing first things first?
5. Are there individuals who are regularly taking my time because they like to visit? Do something about this.
6. What would I gain by coming to work earlier and getting work done without interruptions?
7. Am I spending too much time on low-priority items at work? Be honest with yourself.
8. I will try to meet in the other person's office because it is much easier to leave than to ask someone to leave my office if they just want to chat.
9. I will try to think of each day at work as the last day before going on vacation. Think about this seriously.

How much time can you realistically free up by taking these and other actions? Is it enough? What is your goal?

If your time problem has to do with organizations or other personal commitments, consider making a similar list for analysis.

Remember, it is up to you to choose how you spend your time. Since you are the one making these choices, why not make good choices for you and your family? Say to yourself, "If it is to be, it is up to me."

 Involve your spouse, a family member or a friend in your analysis. Help him or her do the same for their time analysis.

58

CELEBRATING

Take Me Out to the Ball Game

Know the joy of the game.

Barry Bonds has broken Hank Aaron's record with home run number 756. No doubt, a terrific accomplishment. He did it and it is now in the record book. One can challenge how it happened and whether it is a fair comparison with Hank Aaron's feat, or Babe Ruth's 714 or even Willie May's 660.

Times and conditions are different. But aren't times and conditions always different with all types of records? A record is a record is a record. But with this record, is there joy— the same kind of joy as when Babe Ruth had the record and when Hank Aaron overtook Ruth? I don't think so.

Is there joy in Mudville?

I don't think there is as much joy as there should be. This is probably because high salaries, labor disputes, big business, television, high ticket prices, drugs, gambling and many other things have changed the game.

It is not close at all to the fun pick-up games we played, or professional games we watched in which the players were having fun and it was a game. Today it is a big, serious business. This, however, does not take away from Barry Bonds and his new record.

Even so, baseball is still baseball, and isn't it still fun to sing?

Take me out to the ball game,
Take me out with the crowd.
Buy me some peanuts and Cracker Jack,
I don't care if I never get back,
Let me root, root, root for the home team,

If they don't win it's a shame.
For it's one, two, three strikes, you're out,
At the old ball game.

Many of us have played baseball in our younger days, and we know the joy of the game. It is not a boring, slow-moving game when you are playing. It is full of anticipation and excitement.

Did you know the song "Take Me Out to the Ball Game" was written by Jack Norworth and put to music by Albert Von Tilzer in 1908? One day, when Norworth was riding a New York City subway train, he spotted a sign that said, "Ballgame Today at the Polo Grounds." Some baseball-related lyrics popped into his head. Despite the fact that neither Norworth nor Tilzer had ever been to a baseball game at the time the song was written, it is one of the most widely performed songs in America. You would have thought it had been composed by someone who had played and loved the game.

Baseball definitely has been an important part of many Americans' lives over the years, and so many have experienced joy while playing, watching or listening to games.

Baseball has highs and lows, joy and sorrow and, oftentimes, it is difficult to think of it as a game. Think of poor Casey:

The sneer is gone from Casey's lip, his teeth are clenched in hate;
He pounds with cruel violence his bat upon the plate.
And now the pitcher holds the ball, and now he lets it go,
And now the air is shattered by the force of Casey's blow.

Oh, somewhere in this favored land the sun is shining bright;
The band is playing somewhere, and somewhere hearts are light;
And somewhere men are laughing and somewhere children shout,
But there is no joy in Mudville—mighty Casey has struck out.

Did you know there is more to this story? Let me tell you about it, because it has to do with joy and we all want this in our lives.

Casey's Revenge, by Grantland Rice (1906), gives Casey another chance against the pitcher who had struck him out in the original story. In this version, Rice cites the nickname "Strike-Out Casey," hence the influence on Stengel's name. Casey's team is down three runs by the last of the ninth, and once again Casey is down to two strikes, with the bases full this time. However, he connects, and the final stanza reads:

Oh, somewhere in this favored land dark clouds may hide the sun;
And somewhere bands no longer play and children have no fun;
And somewhere over blighted loves there hangs a heavy pall;
But Mudville hearts are happy now—for Casey hit the ball.

Baseball is a wonderful game to play, to watch, to remember, to celebrate successes and, yes, to experience new records as they are broken. Baseball is our game with a wonderful history and prospects for a wonderful future for our young people to experience as have we.

Take someone you love out to the ball game.

59

CELEBRATING

Be Able to Say You Did It Your Way

Present and future opportunities are there.

Do you sometimes speculate about life and what would have happened if you had done this or done that? Did you take enough risks, or too few? How about time spent with the family and friends? Should it have been more? Did you have the right education and attend the right schools? At one time or another, it is common to have all these questions and more.

For many of these kinds of questions, we probably will never know the answers—or will we someday? Will we be able sometime to look at a timeline of our life and see the many options that were available and where each of them would have led? Maybe this will be possible, but if you have the choice, would you really want to see all this? Would it bring joy, or sorrow, and for what purpose?

What we do know is that we have choices now and the younger you are the more choices you have. There are benefits to being able to look back and think about what has happened, what you wish had happened and what you wish had not happened. This looking back should be a positive analysis, because there is the opportunity to make changes that can happen today and tomorrow.

Note that I said some of these things, because as an example, I really would like to play third base for a major league baseball team. I know this isn't going to happen in this lifetime, and if playing in the majors meant giving up something that I love today, I wouldn't want to do it. I think I will wait for my own "Field of Dreams." I hope some of my friends will join me (I get third base).

There are things that can be done both now and in the future that will result in happiness and rewards for you and those whom you love. And best of all, they don't require giving up anything that has already been accomplished or attained.

It might be spending more time with friends. It might be writing that book you have always wanted to write. It very likely could involve your church and your relationship with God.

I think the goal should be to be ready for what the future holds. It would be great to be prepared to take advantage of all the opportunities as they become available.

Frank Sinatra told about this as he sang "My Way":

And now, the end is here
And so I face the final curtain
My friend, I'll say it clear
I'll state my case, of which I'm certain
I've lived a life that's full
I traveled each and every highway
And more, much more than this, I did it my way.

Regrets, I've had a few
But then again, too few to mention
I did what I had to do and saw it through without exemption
I planned each charted course, each careful step along the byway
And more, much more than this, I did it my way.

I've loved, I've laughed and cried
I've had my fill, my share of losing
And now, as tears subside, I find it all so amusing
To think I did all that
And may I say, not in a shy way,
Oh, no, oh, no, not me, I did it my way.

For what is a man, what has he got?
If not himself, then he has naught
To say the things he truly feels and not the words of one who kneels
The record shows I took the blows and did it my way.

Something to think about: Take actions and share with those whom you love. And, yes, be able to say, "I did it my way."

Sing to yourself "My Way."
Let the words be fitting for you.

60

Hanging Around

Is the monkey on your back cute or a conflict?

A number of years ago, there was an article in the *Harvard Business Review* about monkeys in business.

I am not an avid reader of the *Harvard Business Review,* because most articles are written by people who are too smart. However, this issue had an article that I could actually understand and I could relate to its message.

It seems that almost everyone has a few monkeys that they carry around on their shoulders. No one really likes to have these monkeys hanging around. You don't go out and buy them as pets, and you certainly don't adopt them. They are given to you. Some have a few monkeys and some have lots of them.

Some of the monkeys are cute and don't cause too much trouble, but some people's monkeys are mean and seem to thrive on confusion, dissention, criticism and pessimism. These are the ones that are always hungry, feeding on the time and energy of as many carriers as they can.

You see, a monkey is a problem. It might be a missed delivery, a product problem, an unhappy customer, personnel problems, union issues, safety issues, computer problems, sexual harassment, and many other problems. Some monkeys are small and some are quite large. Some are light and some are heavy. Some are young and some are old. Some come and go and some are always there.

Monkeys don't always stay at the workplace. Many like to come home with their carrier and continue to be monkeys all day and night long. Sometimes, these work monkeys join together with personal monkeys to really monkey things up.

What do you do with monkeys? How do you get rid of monkeys? First, it is important to know your own monkeys by name. Which one is the biggest monkey causing the most trouble? It is good to know this monkey well and to deal with him, because he stirs up the other monkeys and makes them do things they wouldn't normally do.

Second would be to make a list of all your monkeys, with names, and list them in order from how mean they are to how little they bother you.

Now that you know your monkeys, you need to decide what to do with them. You can deal with them yourself or you can give them away to someone else. The same is true with others at work and at home: You can let someone else give you their monkeys or you can help them deal with their own monkeys.

As an example at work, consider the sales correspondent who goes to his supervisor because he has an unhappy customer. The unhappy customer is the monkey. The supervisor can tell the sales correspondent not to worry about it, because he will call the customer and take care of it. Here the supervisor is taking the sales correspondent's monkey and the monkey happily jumps from one set of shoulders to another. Or the supervisor can counsel and encourage the correspondent to call the customer directly. In this case, the correspondent keeps his monkey, but goes away with a viable plan for communication with the customer.

As a personal life example, consider some relative or friend who might have a monkey that is a money problem. If you give that person money, you are taking his monkey. If you help him work out his problem, you are helping him or her to get rid of the monkey.

The best advice in dealing with monkeys is not to take other people's monkeys and, likewise, not to give your monkeys to others. Make the monkeys go away and find their own zoo.

Help a friend or relative get rid of a monkey.

61

COACHING

Plan the Work and Work the Plan

Have a plan when looking for a job.

One of my dad's favorite sayings was, "Plan the work and work the plan." As a youth, I was always too busy and in too much of a hurry to take the time to plan. I just wanted to get on with it, and besides, planning is hard work.

Dad was also one to do the A, B, C thing, which is making lists, prioritizing, and using time-management tools. I guess maybe I did learn some things from dear old Dad, because I now do believe in planning before starting the work. I find it is effective to make lists of pros and cons or lists of things to do—in fact all kinds of lists.

So, let's take Dad's advice and plan the work and work the plan with the information available to you when searching for a new job:

Plan the Work

- What types of jobs would you enjoy doing in which your strengths and experience would make you a valuable employee? Recognize that these jobs don't have to satisfy your needs and qualifications 100% of the time. Realistically, around 80% of the time should be spent doing what you are good at and enjoy doing.
- Once you have decided what types of jobs are right for you, determine which companies or organizations have these jobs available.
- Prepare your résumé, highlighting your strengths and the type of job you are seeking. Ask for help here if needed:

  - Be honest in preparing your résumé.

- Be selective in planning distribution of the résumé. This way, it is possible to customize it for the specific job you want and the company you are contacting. It takes a little more time and effort, but is worth it.
- Try to show where you can add value to the company by knowing about the company and perhaps where they have "pains."
- Check, check and check again to make sure you don't have typos or poor grammar. Get some professional help here if necessary.
- Keep it brief—probably not more than two pages. Does the résumé convey your message? If you were the company, would you want to interview you?

- Prepare a cover letter:

  - Include all necessary information: name, address, phone number, e-mail address.
  - Direct the letter to the appropriate individual at the company. Make sure the name is correct, complete and spelled correctly.
  - Tell them why you are sending the letter and résumé to them. Be specific.
  - Ask for an interview; this is your goal.
  - Proofread your letter. Have others proofread it also. A cover letter should always have correct spelling and correct grammar. Don't let a silly mistake in your letter eliminate you from a possible interview.

Work the Plan

- Do networking to find out if any of your friends know someone at the companies or organizations you are interested in interviewing. A friend of a friend is what you are looking for here—someone who can place a call and recommend you for an interview.
- Don't just send your cover letter and résumé to the company. Even a brilliantly prepared cover letter and résumé have little chance of getting attention if they just arrive in the mail. At a minimum, call the individual in charge of human resources or personnel and tell them you are interested in their company and would like to send them your résumé. If you get a chance to visit over the phone, great; if not, you will have made a contact and can refer to this in your cover letter.
- Hand-deliver your cover letter and résumé in person. If you don't get a chance to meet the human resources manager, take the opportunity to meet the receptionist. Try to make a good impression on her. Dress as though you were going to an interview.
- Follow up in about a week with a phone call to see what additional information they might want. Mention that your schedule is flexible for interviews and that you would be willing to make several visits if more than one individual would be involved in the

interviewing process. Sometimes the problem with getting an interview is one of scheduling the right people.

- Don't put all your eggs in one basket. Look for a number of opportunities.

Good advice is to be patient. Don't jump at the first job offer that comes your way unless you are sure it is what you want. Be positive and optimistic, especially in interviews and in written communications.

Be upbeat, positive and optimistic during the job search.

62

Beware the Ides of March

It's time to celebrate spring.

Spring officially began March 20, and with the beginning of spring, so many thoughts come to mind about past years and the fresh beginning of this time of year.

Alfred Lord Tennyson wrote, "In the spring a young man's fancy lightly turns to thoughts of love." It is also a time to think about spring flowers, new projects, the beginning of the baseball season and, of course, the final four in basketball. Spring has sprung, and this usually means happy thoughts and plans, as it should. It is a wonderful time of year—fresh, bright and cheerful.

I think it is also a time when one could reflect on the saying, "Beware the Ides of March." What does this mean and what does this have to do with the beginning of spring? "Beware the Ides of March" is a famous saying from Shakespeare's *Julius Caesar*.

Caesar:
Who is it in the press that calls on me?
I hear a tongue shriller than all the music
Cry 'Caesar!' Speak! Caesar is turn'd to hear.

Soothsayer:
Beware the Ides of March.

Caesar:
What man is that?

Brutus:
A soothsayer bids you beware the Ides of March.

March 15 is the Ides of March, which is the day that Julius Caesar was assassinated in the senate in 44 BC. This could be considered a very unlucky day for him, and this saying a kind of warning, as it was to Caesar.

To us, this could be a reminder to think about this present year, which is now almost three months old, and all that must be accomplished. Is it a warning or a wake-up call saying that we should get started, since precious time is flying by? To us, it is not about death, as it was to Caesar, but about life and progress.

"Beware the Ides of March" might just be a well-known saying, a kind of superstition that has no real meaning, like so many of those we know but tend to ignore:

- Friday the Thirteenth is unlucky
- Walking under a ladder
- Black Cats
- Breaking a glass while proposing a toast
- Getting out of bed left foot first
- Breaking a mirror
- Opening an umbrella indoors
- Stepping on cracks in the sidewalk

Hardly anyone believes that if you break a mirror you will have seven years of bad luck, or that opening an umbrella indoors will bring bad luck. But, many do worry about them. So, why would some worry about these popular superstitions and not about the Ides of March? I think the answer is that these are superstitions, nothing more, just plain old superstitions that don't mean anything. Now, "Beware the Ides of March" is another matter. It is old and probably has lost its original meaning to most people; it is basically ignored, but still famous. Shakespeare's way with words keeps it alive in modern-day memory—the saying, but not the meaning.

In his day, Caesar looked at "Beware the Ides of March" differently from our perception of it today. I think we should look at it as a positive challenge and motivator to move forward with the optimistic plans and goals that we have established for the year. Spring should be the time of year to celebrate what has been accomplished thus far and a call to step it up where we are behind in our goals, projects and plans.

There is no reason to fear the saying, "Beware the Ides of March," because we are moving into spring with enthusiasm and optimism. We don't need this warning anymore this year.

Take the opportunity to read some Shakespeare this week. You will enjoy it.

63

COACHING

Positives First

There will be enough time to cover negatives.

Do you know people who always seem to be looking for the negatives and
the positives? You probably also know those who only look at the positives a
consider the possible low wires. Both of these ways of analyzing situations or o
present problems to many companies and in personal situations.

What is needed is the right balance of being positive, first of all, and the
looking at the risks or low wires. The positives have to outweigh the negatives in t

At one time, I was involved with an organization that was very negativ
answer was always no. We did a number of things to change this "no" attitud
reading Norman Vincent Peale's book, *The Power of Positive Thinking,* and Dal
book, *How to Win Friends and Influence People.* The messages in these books h
but not enough. So, what did we do?

We developed an internal mission statement: "Just say yes!" What this m
say "yes" to our customers, "yes" to our sales organization and "yes" to our
Does this make sense, and is it possible to do? The answer is, of course, "yes."

How can you "Just say Yes!" and make it happen? This works when there
attitude. In other words, when the customer asks for something, the answer i
it is necessary to determine what the company must do to make it happen Al
required of the customer.

You see, what is being said to the customer is that, yes, we want to give
they are asking for; that means the parties have to work together to achieve
results. It is forming a "yes" partnership, not a unilateral "yes" commit
approach works because it is based on real customer focus and the devel
customer partners. Care about your customers and they will care about you.

Many have had bosses, or have them now, who look at a situation or oppor
study all the reasons why it won't work, or what can go wrong or what isn't i

it.
to

so
pe

po
wi
pr
pr

th
ca
ne
ou

f they go through their list of ten negative things, there just isn't the time or energy
egin looking at the positives. It's too late then.

Whereas, if you first look at all the good things and decide you want to make
ething happen, it probably will. I believe this is the way to put the negatives in better
spective.

The way to make this happen is to take the lead and make the presentation with all the
itives provided up front. If your boss interrupts with questions about the risks or low
es, tell him or her that it is a good question and will be covered later in the
sentation. It's okay to tell your boss that you intend to tell why you are in favor of this
ject and cover the risks later.

t is much more energizing and definitely more enjoyable to focus on the positives;
re will be time and energy for covering the negatives or low wires later. This is not the
e if the focus is, first, on the negatives and reasons for not doing something. Covering
atives first is draining and tiring. Negatives just seem to beat you up and take the life
of you and your presentation. So make sure positives are first and negatives are last.

If someone is being negative, encourage
them to look for the positives in the
situation.

64

Mentoring

It's an invaluable experience for everyone involved.

A previous action discussed mentoring, what it is and the origin of the word. There were several mentor definitions given. I think they could be summed up by saying a mentor is a role model who is a wise and trusted counselor or teacher.

In a recent small group meeting, we discussed mentors we have had in the past. It was interesting, because some have had long-term mentors and some have had none. There were also examples of parents trying to fill the role of mentors, but this is very different. All in our group agreed that having a mentor and being a mentor are positive and important in life.

Why become a mentor?

Many people answer this question in terms of how much the young benefit from having a mentor, and this is correct. It is also correct that the mentor benefits, perhaps even more, by this act of volunteering. Isn't this so often the case?

The mentor benefits by...

- Receiving a feeling of fulfillment as a result of caring
- Receiving a significant purpose in life
- Gaining a new friend
- Providing the opportunity to be creative
- Using listening and problem-solving skills
- Achieving satisfaction by making a difference in someone's life
- Providing an outlet to teach from experience
- Providing a means of giving back to the community

When I was with ABB, the president of the company, headquartered in Zurich, Switzerland, started a reverse mentoring program. He required the top 400 managers in the company to meet for at least an hour a week with a young employee whom each would select.

The goal of the reverse mentoring program was to have the young teach the old how to use computers and the Internet. This was having the AC employees working with the BC employees. You know this stands for a generation of "After Computer" individuals and a different generation of "Before Computer" managers.

There were also some references to those with grey hair. This was not very kind, but it was accurate.

The program was very effective, and we did become much more proficient in using our computers. I think this reverse mentoring program, learning about computers, was actually the secondary reason for the program. I believe our president felt we weren't in touch with the younger generation. We didn't understand their thinking, their expectations or what was important to them. He was right, because times have changed, employees have changed and management needed to change also. This program demonstrated the value to both parties of the mentoring process.

Why have a mentor?

There are many good reasons for having a mentor; I can't think of reasons for not having one, can you? Here are some thoughts on pros for mentoring:

- Think about the benefits of having an experienced tour guide. You can read books and study about where you are going, but how much more valuable it is to be with someone who has been there and will guide you. This is what a mentor does. A mentor guides you in areas that he knows you have not yet experienced.
- A mentor is a sounding board—someone with whom to discuss "what if" scenarios and ideas you might have. There is a real need for someone you can trust who will listen to what you are thinking without feeling threatened.
- A mentor can help you develop a vision and will encourage you to think bigger.
- A mentor will encourage risk-taking after discussing the pros and cons of significant opportunities.
- A mentor seeks to encourage the development of your gifts, while seeking to protect you from making costly mistakes.

If your company does not have a mentoring program, you might consider suggesting they give it a try. Perhaps for some particular reason or need, you could suggest an initiative such as the ABB reverse mentoring program.

You know it is okay to ask someone to be your mentor just the same as it would be okay to offer your time as a mentor. You might just say you have been thinking about someone who mentored you and you would like to do the same with someone else.

Mentoring is definitely a win-win kind of opportunity. There are so many benefits for the mentor and the protégé. If you are presently not a mentor, consider being one, and if you do not have a mentor, consider finding one.

Encourage younger family members to find a mentor.

65

I Have Never Walked in His Shoes

Where has he been and where is he going?

How often have you wondered why someone did something that you considered to be dumb, or very inconsiderate or out of place? Or why someone acted the way they did in a certain situation? Or why he or she said what they said at that particular time? And you think to yourself, I would never say something like that or behave in such a manner.

Or would you?

It is the experiences, environment and associations that you have had during your life that lead you to think and respond as you do. There is nothing really magical about it—it is just the way it is.

Generally, we don't even think about how we view others and their behavior—we just do it. Seldom do we take the time to consider that maybe there were other factors or influences that made the person do what he or she did. Maybe knowing all the background information would change your opinion of how the person acted or what they said. Maybe this is so because we haven't walked in their shoes.

I thought about this just the other day when someone asked me at what stage of my life I had started to feel confident and comfortable in meetings with high-level people. It was an unusual query, I thought, so I asked the individual to clarify his question.

He explained that when he is invited to meetings such as the one we were attending, he isn't sure whether he has been invited to be a part of the committee because of his job or because of who he is personally.

I mentally put myself in his position in order to understand his concern. I wanted to empathize with him so that I could respond in a meaningful way. Then, I realized that I hadn't walked in his shoes, so how could I really know how deep or serious his question might be and what kind of answer would be helpful?

His question, and the way it was asked, should not be taken lightly. This was not meant to be just small talk.

I used an example, referred to in another action, of visiting one of our ABB companies in Europe where the managing director asked one of our people, "Who are you and why are you here?" It was a good question, very direct; it started the meeting in a positive and productive way. So, my advice to the young man who asked the question about being confident in meetings was to consider the question, "Who are you and why are you here?" He is walking in his own shoes, so he is the one to answer this question.

Just the other night, a good friend was discussing some family matters and asked me what I thought about what he was doing. Again, I realized I couldn't answer that question because I hadn't walked in his shoes. You just don't know all that has happened over time—all the background and feelings associated with the matter.

So, it wouldn't be fair or reasonable to answer a question like that without knowing everything that my friend knew. That is what I told him. I respect him and what he does, and I think that is what really counts, not my speculating on what should be done—without walking in his shoes.

Someone once asked me, "If you haven't walked in another's shoes, how can you possibly know where he is coming from and where he is going?" I think that is a wonderful question that we need to be reminded of on a regular basis.

When asked by anyone to give advice, before answering, consider whether it is necessary to have walked in his or her shoes.

66

COMMUNICATING

Giving Up on Grammar?

Speed vs. Style

I wonder if our society is more or less giving up on the use of proper grammar. You hear the wrong words spoken every day on the radio and TV, and newspapers aren't much better. Is this a problem, or is it something that we should learn to live with and just accept?

In a few years, who will be left who really cares about grammar anyway? So, today, why make a fuss over such a small thing as me and Joe discussing our poor grammar and your's to?

Okay, okay, I realize that everyone knows it's "Joe and I," or do they? Would you be happier with "Joe and me"? Does this make you want to pull out your red marker to change "to" to "too" and "your's" to "yours"? Of course, it does.

I have a friend who loves proper grammar and, I believe, really does have a fixation about proofreading the newspaper and articles. I think this is his hobby, his way of relaxing instead of doing Sudoku or crossword puzzles. He even sends copies of my articles back to me with corrections, which by the way, I really do appreciate. He is very good at what he does.

Today, with all the young people doing text messaging with abbreviations and, obviously, no thought at all to grammar, what should we expect? The same is true of e-mail correspondence and the Internet. It is speed that counts much more than using the right words or proper sentence structure. Maybe they're right. Perhaps it is better to communicate with fewer and shorter words. Why is there a need to use capital letters, periods and other forms of punctuation? it is, for the most part, just a waste of valuable time

How about picking out a few examples of poor grammar and word usage that are the most annoying and let our newscasters, talk show hosts and newspaper reporters know we expect them to set reasonable examples for their listeners and readers? A few examples follow:

- Don't say me and Joe. Don't ever start out with "me" and someone. Putting proper grammar aside, if for no other reason, just remember it is polite to mention the other person's name first.
- The word "got" is misused often. He's got the media on his side and she's got them against her, for example. We all know he "has" the media on his side and she "has" them against her. We also know what this example is all about, don't we? "Got" has got to go and so has ... oh, well, let's see what happens. It will be a few years yet before we know.

Some words are overused to the extent that we basically want to stop listening to them. Actually, we do stop listening. Basically, this is the message here—that people who start most sentences with the word basically actually get boring. So, think about helping those who use basically and actually too much. A way of doing this would be to ask nicely, "What do you mean by basically?" Actually, this might help. Ouch!

Lie and lay are often used in the wrong way, but does that really matter so much? You know what the person means, so let a sleeping dog lie or lay. Let the dog do whatever he wants, especially if he is big and bites. Remember, chickens lay eggs and people lie down.

Words can be fun and so can grammar. Good speakers use the right words and generally have good grammar. Sometimes, this alone impresses and influences the audience. Sometimes, it doesn't, because most important of all is not the usage of words or proper grammar. What really matters is what's being said and the actions taken to support the words.

Pass on some thoughts and examples about grammar and word usage to young members of your family.

67

◎〜◎〜◎ CARING ◎〜◎〜◎

Is This Heaven?

If you build it, they will come.

Ray Kinsella, in the movie *Field of Dreams,* keeps hearing "If you build it, he will come." He doesn't know what this means at first, but later becomes convinced that he needs to plow under his corn crops and build a baseball diamond on his farm. Ray is a novice farmer who is struggling to make ends meet, so giving up his choice land is a serious thing to do.

One of the first people to come onto his diamond was Shoeless Joe Jackson, who was banned from baseball for his part in throwing the 1919 World Series. It was Shoeless Joe who told Ray what "If you build it, he will come" means. **He,** in this case, is Ray's deceased father, John Kinsella, a man who loved baseball, the Chicago White Sox and Shoeless Joe Jackson. Ray built this field so that he would come.

Ray always regretted giving up baseball and playing catch with his dad when he was 14. Now, on the field of dreams that he built, he has the opportunity to play catch again with his dad. The film's underlying themes are the fulfillment of dreams and how people can overcome any regrets they may have about the life choices they make.

John Kinsella asks his son, Ray, "Is this heaven?" Ray answers, "It's Iowa." John says, "Iowa! I could have sworn this was heaven." "Is there a heaven?" Ray asks. John tells him, "Oh, yeah. It's a place where dreams come true." Ray, viewing his farm, his wife and daughter says, "Maybe this is heaven."

There are other dreams that come true in this movie. It is more than a baseball movie. It is a movie about dreams coming true. Maybe you have a dream about visiting the Field of Dreams. It is possible, you know. The Field of Dreams is located in Heaven—no, I mean in Iowa. It is in Dyersville, Iowa, which is in northeastern Iowa, 170 miles from Des Moines and 210 miles from Chicago.

"If you build it, they will come." The first visitors arrived on May 5, 1989. People have come from all corners of the world. People are magically drawn to Dyersville for reasons they can't explain. At the Field of Dreams, they say the best thing about the place is what isn't there; instead of providing images and dreams, it is content to be a mere stage. It is up to each visitor to provide the drama and cast that he or she desires.

This baseball diamond is in the middle of cornfields in Iowa. How you take advantage of the opportunity of being there reminds me of what our grandson told us about our visit to Mexico: "Great, but we will have to make our own fun." That's what is wonderful about the Field of Dreams. You can play catch with someone special to you, run the bases, hit fly balls to the outfield, do infield practice, pitch batting practice or just sit in the bleachers and think about your own dreams. You make your own fun.

If you are going to Dyersville, Iowa, be sure to remember to take your favorite bat, ball and glove. Most important is to take that special person who will be a part of your dream come true.

If you don't plan to go to Dyersville, Iowa, soon, plan to go to another special Field of Dreams where you can make some dreams come true for you or someone close to you. It doesn't have to be Iowa—it can be heaven in some other location.

 Decide to make a visit to your special "Field of Dreams" this summer.

68

CARING

Give Them Cake

Do more for others than is expected.

A famous quotation from Charles Dickens' *A Tale of Two Cities* is quoted both correctly and incorrectly, but the real meaning of the quotation remains the same. One way is: "The people are asking for bread, give them cake." Another way is: "The people ask for bread, let them eat cake."

Legend has it that when the queen of France, Marie Antoinette, was told that the poor people had no bread to eat, she responded, "Let them eat cake." There is some doubt that she actually said this, but there is no question that in 1793, at the height of the French Revolution, she was executed.

The easiest for me to relate to is, "If someone asks for bread, give them cake." No matter how the quotation is stated, if the intention is that you do more than what is expected, then it has to be okay. You are not going to lose your head over an incorrectly worded quotation. We no longer use the guillotine.

I know a number of companies feel very strongly about the meaning behind this message, because the short quotation is easy to understand and remember. Giving cake is important, but it is not necessary for all meals. This means that when the customers ask for bread, give them cake. But you don't have to give them "cake" for "meals" that aren't so important.

Determining the right meals, which could be described as significant needs, wants or expectations, is not hard to determine. The best way to find out the most important needs of a customer is simply to ask. Several local companies have done this through surveys and interviews. These companies found the same results. Most important to their customers was on-time deliveries. Next was short delivery times, followed by doing business with someone they could trust. Consistently delivering the product on time, or even a little early, was the top priority. This was giving the customer cake.

Developing an easily understood marketing plan for an organization or a business can be complicated. But developing a cake plan is not. The key is to find out what's most important to the customers; then determine how to give them more than they expect.

They expect bread, but your marketing plan should be designed to give them cake. If you give them cake, not only will they want to do business with you, they will tell their friends about your great service, deliveries, communications or whatever flavor your cake might be.

This marketing appeal might be applied to retirement homes. They have marketing people who work hard to fill the vacant apartments. They promote safety, security, activities, clean and attractive facilities, affordable accommodations and so forth.

These are all important, of course, but what is most important to the seniors living there and what do they talk about most? You're right—it's the food. And, usually, it's complaining about the food. If they are complaining about the food to their neighbors, you can be sure they are negative to prospective residents.

Just think how easy it would be to fill the vacant apartments if the retirement home had a reputation for having the best food in town. So, the analysis should target what it would cost to have excellent food and service and how profitable a full or almost full facility would be, even with increased costs for high-quality meals. The same is true for country clubs. Think about that.

We know of a family whose daughter is an outstanding swimmer. She had full scholarship offers and could choose to go to almost any university in the country. She chose UCLA because the athletic dorm has a reputation for having the best food in the country. They have a good coach and program also, but this girl said she chose UCLA because of the food.

Now, wouldn't excellent food in a retirement home be even more of a selling point than at a university?

Let them eat cake.

If a friend or neighbor is asking for bread, give them cake.

69

Living on Lombardi Time

Adhere to this simple rule and never be late again.

Why do organizations and businesses feel it is necessary to have so many lengthy meetings? Think of all the time that is consumed in meetings that could be spent doing more productive things. We are a meeting society, and even with advanced technology for communication, meetings just haven't changed very much over the years.

Next year's meetings probably aren't going to be very different unless we take some positive actions to improve them. It can be done. The gain in productivity and the freeing up of valuable time will make some changes well worth the effort. Think of it this way: If you're going to take the time to go to meetings, why not make them as productive as possible?

Here are a few tips to consider for meeting changes. The first one comes from the great Hall of Fame football coach of the Green Bay Packers, Vince Lombardi. Vince invented a strategy that he recommended to his coaches and players. It came to be known as Lombardi Time, and it embodied a valuable habit that is even more appropriate to us in our daily lives than it was to football players.

Lombardi Time states, "Show up for every important meeting 15 minutes ahead of the scheduled meeting time." The idea is, first and foremost, to ensure that you are always on time for all meetings. Additional benefits from Lombardi Time are the 15 minutes to catch your breath, collect your thoughts and review what you have already decided you want to accomplish in the meeting. Take this time before the meeting to go over your strategy for making it as successful as possible.

Stating your belief in Lombardi Time would be a good way to encourage others to be on time for the meeting. I know there are managers who lock the door when it is time to start the meeting. Those who aren't in the room will learn a lesson and you can bet they will become believers of Lombardi Time for future meetings.

It was Lombardi who said, "If it doesn't matter who wins or loses, then why do they keep score?" Someone should be keeping score on who arrives on time and who is late for important meetings. This might determine the winners and losers.

The motto of the Boy Scouts of America is "Be Prepared." "Be prepared for what?" someone once asked Baden-Powell, the founder of scouting. "Why, for any old thing," said Baden-Powell.

The training that scouts receive helps them to be prepared. When someone has an accident, scouts are prepared because of their first-aid instruction. Because of lifesaving practice, a scout might be able to save a non-swimmer who is in trouble.

Being prepared is more than being ready for emergencies. Baden-Powell's idea was that all scouts should prepare themselves to become productive citizens and to give happiness to other people. He wanted each scout to be ready in mind and body for any struggles, and to meet with a strong heart whatever challenges might lie ahead.

Just think how productive meetings would be if all who attended were truly prepared. You can't have meetings with only scouts who have been taught to be prepared, but you can make sure you are prepared. You can also make sure the objectives of the meeting are clear and understood in advance. You can influence this action, even if it isn't your meeting, by simply asking questions before the meeting.

It should be easy to remember just two things when you schedule a meeting or are invited to attend one: First would be to remember Lombardi Time; second would be to remember the Boy Scout motto, "Be Prepared." This is basic—be on time and be prepared.

Practice Lombardi Time except when invited to someone's home.

70

Don't Shrug It Off

Some say *Atlas Shrugged* is about today.

Did you know that one of my favorite books, *Atlas Shrugged,* is selling at a faster rate today than at any time during its 51-year history? Ayn Rand died more than a quarter of a century ago, yet her name appears regularly in discussions of our current economic turmoil.

There's a reason. In *Atlas Shrugged,* Rand tells the story of the U.S. economy crumbling under the weight of crushing government intervention and regulation. Does this sound familiar?

Atlas Shrugged is, no doubt, a very special book. Ayn Rand and *Atlas Shrugged* have many loyal and enthusiastic fans. Some are even members of clubs and organizations who correspond and meet regularly to compare the book with our current government direction. The goal is entertainment, of course, but also to help prevent another *Atlas Shrugged* ending.

Many experiences are told about this book and those who have read it. Several happened to me:

About ten years ago, while on a cruise with friends of ours, we spent a day in Barbados. Instead of going to the beach with our traveling companions, I visited an old friend from York, Pennsylvania, who has a manufacturing company on the island. During our time together that day, I asked him why he named his company Galt Controls. He told me that during a particularly trying time in his life, he was reading Rand's book, *Atlas Shrugged.* He believed he got the answers he was searching for from this book, and decided to start his own company. This led him to name the company Galt Controls. I really appreciated hearing this explanation, because I knew the answer to "Who is John Galt?"

I later joined our friends on the beach and shared this story about Galt Controls. I also mentioned that I would like to read *Atlas Shrugged* again. One of our friends went over to his backpack and pulled out a brand new copy of the book. He said he really didn't know why he had bought it at an airport bookstore while waiting for his plane in Detroit. His buying this book and having it on a beach in Barbados was quite a coincidence—or was it?

It was unbelievable the number of people who stopped to talk to me on airplanes when they saw I was reading this wonderful book. It is a special group who have a kind of respect for those who appreciate the writing of Ayn Rand.

On one trip, returning home, for some unknown reason I checked my bag. Usually, this would be a carry-on bag. While waiting for my plane, I realized that my copy of *Atlas Shrugged* was in the checked bag.

I returned to the ticket counter and asked the man who had checked me in if I could get my bag back. He said no—it was on its way to the plane and there wasn't anything he could do to get it back. I told him that my book was in the bag, and I wanted to continue reading it on this long flight.

He suggested that I try the local bookstore. I told him I had already done that, but they didn't have the book in stock. He asked the name of the book, and I told him it was *Atlas Shrugged*. He looked at me in a rather strange way and quietly asked me what my bag looked like. I described it, and he told me to wait there for a few minutes. He returned shortly with my book. I think when he heard *Atlas Shrugged,* he knew what he had to do. This is amazing, wouldn't you say?

I believe *Atlas Shrugged* people do things like this because they know the kind of people who read the book, and they know they would do the same for them.

Today it would be my hope that President Obama and others in Congress take the time to read *Atlas Shrugged.* I think it might help. They should be asking the question, "Who is John Galt and where is he when we need him so much?"

I'm sure many today are wishing more of our politicians and our president were people who would read *Atlas Shrugged.*

Read *Atlas Shrugged* or another favorite book.

71

Reflect, Restore, Refresh

Take time to reflect, restore, refresh and renew.

At the halfway point each year it seems that only a few months have passed. Even so, we can think about where we are today in a positive and optimistic way, knowing that half the year is still available for reflecting, restoring and refreshing. Is the year half over, or is half the year left to accomplish what is important?

This is going to be an interesting year with many opportunities, and yet, with many uncertainties. It is a political year in which both sides will be saying and doing things that could be very harmful to our country, our economy and our security. With this kind of environment, it seems likely that many companies will be taking a very conservative approach to business expansion and investment. Some companies might even be cutting back on their workforce in anticipation of the need to reduce costs during the year.

I hope this speculation about the second half of the year is not sounding too negative or pessimistic. It is not meant to be. The purpose is, in a small way, to act as a wake-up call for you or a family member to reflect on what has happened during the first half of the year. It should then be followed with positive actions to refresh and restore during the second half of the year.

How do you reflect on what has happened during the first six months? First, you should think about your job or your business. How is it really going? Are you completely confident about your position and your security in your present position? If your company has to cut back 10% to 15% of the employees, is it possible that your name might be on that list? Be completely objective and honest in your analysis of where you line up in this kind of ranking.

Your reflection should include your own analysis of how good an employee you are. Do you feel your boss or supervisor and his or her boss like you and appreciate the work you do? Or, do you really know? With the uncertainties mentioned earlier, it is not a good time to be risking losing your job if there are things you can do now to prevent this from happening.

The following is a list of suggestions you might consider for yourself, for family members or friends:

Ten suggestions for restoring and renewing

1. Commit to being early for work and plan to stay later than the normal quitting time. It doesn't have to be much, but make sure you are not arriving late for work and leaving early.
2. Don't spend time on personal business during work time. This also means not using your company computer for personal e-mails or the Internet for other than business purposes. You know all of this can be tracked and has been used in numerous cases as grounds for termination.
3. Don't use the company telephone for personal long distance calls. These also are listed and can be easily identified. Some personal local calls are necessary, but don't make a habit of using company time for your personal calls. If you have to make a long-distance call, use your cell phone.
4. Take the right lunch breaks; stay within the company policy for lunch and official breaks during the day.
5. Make it a practice to complete your assignments early and do a little more than what is expected. Give it that extra effort.
6. Ask questions if there is any doubt about the assignment or what is expected of you. If you are still not completely sure, put your understanding in writing as a confirmation.
7. Be especially kind and considerate of fellow workers during the balance of the year.
8. Have a good time at work. Enjoy yourself and help others to do the same. Have a sense of humor. Don't take yourself too seriously.
9. Use logic and common sense in all dealings with others at work.
10. Talk to your boss about your performance. Let him or her know that you appreciate having your job and want to make the most of it. What more can you do to become more valuable to the company?

Reflect on your performance after thinking about these ten suggestions for restoring and renewing.

It's time to reflect on the first half of the year and use the balance of the year for restoring and renewing.

72

Where, Oh, Where Did the Hour Go?

We should learn to make the most of our extra time.

How would we remember what to do with our clocks twice a year, in March and November, if someone hadn't thought of "spring ahead, fall back"?

Shortly after we were married and living in Boston, one Sunday in late October, we were looking forward to watching a professional football game. I couldn't find it on television, so I called a friend who knew everything about football: players, teams, statistics and most certainly starting game times. He said, "Don't you realize we just went off daylight-saving time and the kickoff time is two hours away?"

Well, this is when I learned that it was fall back, not fall ahead. I had turned the clock ahead one hour instead of back one hour. This day turned out to be the longest day ever for us and one that we will never forget.

We got one free hour the beginning of November. Having an extra hour in the day is like a gift. Most of us probably take the extra hour for granted, rather than taking advantage of it to do something productive and fun. It suddenly becomes Monday, and there we are back to having just the same number of hours, starting first thing in the morning and ending at night. There wasn't an extra hour to be found anyplace on Monday.

Well, why not? Were we looking in all the wrong places? Wouldn't it be possible each year to take advantage of that extra hour to do special things and keep doing them all during the year, even in daylight-saving time (DST)? It could be done by focusing on time-management practices, doing first things first and recognizing the importance of priorities. Maybe going off daylight-saving time would be a good time to remind ourselves to concentrate on having an extra, very rewarding and productive hour every day.

Benjamin Franklin has so many wonderful sayings and quotations that we like to repeat and relate to our own experiences. One of the best known is, "Early to bed, and early to rise, makes a man healthy, wealthy and wise."

It is written that Benjamin Franklin, while living in Paris, anonymously published a letter suggesting that Parisians economize on candles by rising earlier to use morning sunlight. This 1784 satire proposed taxing shutters, rationing candles, and waking the public by ringing church bells and firing cannons at sunrise. Franklin, although an early riser, did not propose daylight-saving time.

Modern DST was first proposed in 1907 by the English builder William Willett. He conceived DST in 1905 during a pre-breakfast ride, when he observed with dismay how many Londoners slept through a large part of a summer day. An avid golfer, he also disliked cutting short his round of golf at dusk. His solution was to advance the clock during the summer months. He lobbied unsuccessfully for the proposal until his death in 1915.

William Willett would be happy to know that daylight-saving time is now employed in about seventy countries around the world, including almost every major industrialized nation. In the United States, from 1987 through 2006, a daylight-saving time period of almost seven months was in effect from 2 a.m. on the first Sunday in April to 2 a.m. the last Sunday in October.

Today, the country observes a DST period of almost eight months. In 2009, DST is from Sunday, March 14, to Sunday, November 7.

We don't have to wait until November to start taking advantage of having one special, productive and rewarding hour each day. Take that hour now and use it each and every day.

Have a special hour each day starting today.

73

COMMUNICATING

Questions and More Questions

That's a good question, so where's the answer?

We have elected a new president, Barack Obama, and with his election come many unanswered questions. Just think of all the questions there are about what this man is going to do in the near term and during his four or eight years as president. He has said so much and made so many promises during the last two years of campaigning that there just have to be questions.

All the candidates campaigning in the primaries and in the presidential campaign also made many promises to the public about what they would do if they were elected president. It wasn't only Obama who was doing all the talking; it is, however, only Obama who now has to deliver on his promises.

There are so many questions about our economy, our security, our energy dependency, our national debt, our spending and so many more. These are all very difficult and complex questions. No doubt, this president faced many serious challenges, starting with day one.

Who can answer all these important questions and how can they be answered? I heard that there are four ways of responding to questions. See how these fit with your understanding of how to answer questions:

1. There are questions that should be answered categorically, in a straightforward way, with yes or no.
2. There are questions that should be answered with an analytical response in the form of a qualified answer, defining or redefining the terms.
3. There are questions that should be answered with a counter-question.
4. There are questions that should be put aside to be answered at a later date, if at all.

There is also a question that should be answered before the other questions are answered. That question is, "Are campaign statements or promises really promises or are they just words that attract voters?"

Probably all or almost all of the statements or promises made during the campaign would fit into the last three ways to answer a question. Not many would get a straight yes or no during the first 100 days in office.

We all have so many questions. It is natural to have them, but difficult to be patient and understanding. Maybe we really don't want to hear all the answers.

Let's look at what some famous people have said about questions and answers:

If you want a wise answer, ask a reasonable question. Johann Wolfgang Von Goethe

No question is so difficult to answer as that for which the answer is obvious. George Bernard Shaw

An expert knows all the answers—if you ask the right questions. Unknown Source

When someone says, 'That's a good question' you can be sure it's a lot better than the answer you're going to get. Unknown Source

There are no foolish questions and no one becomes a fool until they have stopped asking questions. Unknown Source

To be or not to be that is the question. Whether it is nobler in the mind to suffer the stings and arrows of outrageous fortune, or take up arms against a sea of troubles, and by opposing them, end them. William Shakespeare

Obama and Hamlet are perhaps similar in having the opportunity and need to make difficult and unpopular decisions—thus suffering the stings and arrows of outrageous fortune—or taking up arms against a sea of troubles.

Our new president is going to need all the support he can get, and it is up to the American public to make this happen. However, the president must earn the support of the majority by leading our country in the right way, in the right direction, with the right programs.

Don't ask a question if you're not prepared for the answer.

74

Happy Talk Will Keep Away the Blues

You have to accentuate the positive.

Today we need to hear much more "happy talk." Mostly, we are hearing doom and gloom from our president and the news media all day long. This constant troubling talk is having a severe negative influence on almost all aspects of our daily lives.

Certainly, this is the case with our economy and the stock market. Don't you agree that it's time to look into the future with optimistic programs that will generate positive results? There has been enough time spent blaming others. It is time to move forward and accept responsibility for actions taken today. What we need is some good, old-fashioned happy talk.

> *Happy talk, keep talking happy talk.*
> *Talk about things you like to do.*
> *You got to have a dream,*
> *if you don't have a dream,*
> *How you gonna have a dream come true?*

This is, of course, from *South Pacific*, music by Richard Rodgers and lyrics by Oscar Hammerstein II. Don't you agree that it's time to have some happy talk and re-establish our dreams?

We live in a great country that is blessed with many opportunities. We have so much to be thankful for, including the wisdom of our founding fathers, who have given us the basis and guidelines for running our government. Our job is to elect representatives who will do what they are supposed to do; if they don't, we need to elect others who will. This is on our minds now because there are so many questions about what our government is doing under the umbrella of trying to correct our economic problems.

Everything is not doom and gloom. Just think about all the good things that are happening every day. We need to shift our attention to the rewarding and positive experiences we have and the many opportunities available for us to share and contribute in meaningful ways.

I think about Louis Armstrong's "What a Wonderful World" recording from 1967. This song helps to put things in a better perspective. Read the words and just picture him singing this song:

> *I see trees of green, red roses, too,*
> *I see them bloom for me and for you,*
> *And I think to myself, 'It's a wonderful world.'*
> *I see skies of blue, clouds of white,*
> *The bright blessed days and the dark sacred nights,*
> *And I think to myself, 'What a wonderful world.'*
> *The colors of the rainbow, so bright up in the sky,*
> *Are also on the faces of people passin' by,*
> *I see friends shakin' hands, sayin', 'How do you do?'*
> *They're really sain', 'I love you.'*
> *And I think to myself, 'It's a wonderful world.'*

It is a wonderful world. Of course, there are problems and we have some significant challenges ahead of us, but isn't that always the case? You know that life is good, the future is bright, these dark clouds will pass, so let's take advantage of all we have to enjoy and share with those we love. After all, isn't that what really counts and what is most important? Remember these words from Bing Crosby:

> *You've got to accentuate the positive*
> *Eliminate the negative*
> *Latch on to the affirmative*
> *Don't mess with Mister In-Between.*

Think of favorite songs that help you focus on positive thoughts and eliminate the negative. Sing them to yourself each day and see what happens.

 Sing, sing, sing, sing your favorite songs each day.

75

CARING

For Many, Love Is Spelled T-I-M-E

It's the best day of my life.

How often do you think you can have the "time of your life"? When asked if you had a good time on your vacation or at some event, it is easy to answer with, "Yes, it was great—I had the time of my life." But is it really the time of your life? That would have to mean, chronologically, that each time has to be better than the former and better than all in past years.

No doubt, all of us have had many "time of your life" experiences, and fortunately, we are not questioned on which is best. There is no real reason to rank them for ourselves, but should we consider ranking them as our loved ones and family might? Could it be, sometimes, that our "time of your life" experience is very different for our spouse or family?

I recently read a story from a book titled, *To a Child Love is Spelled T-I-M-E*. The story is about an old man who was looking for a favorite photo of his long gone wife—the love of his life. He was going through old boxes in the attic when he discovered a journal from his grown son's childhood. He could not recall ever having seen it before or even that his son had kept a journal.

Opening the yellowed pages, he glanced over a short reading, and then another followed by another. He could hear the voice of the little boy who had grown up far too fast in this same house. Entry after entry stirred a sentimental hunger in his heart, but it was accompanied by the painful memory that his son's simple recollections of those days were far different from his own.

He remembered that he had kept a daily journal of his business activities over the years. He found his old journal and placed the two beside each other. He opened his own journal to a page on which he had written, "Wasted the whole day fishing with Jimmy. Didn't catch a thing." With a deep sigh and a shaking hand, he took Jimmy's journal and found the boy's entry for the same day, June 4. Large scrawling letters, pressed deeply into the paper, read, "Went fishing with my dad. Best day of my life."

Maybe it's too late for this old man to do anything about how time was spent with his son in the past or the numerous opportunities missed. Or maybe not. Perhaps there is still time for him to be together with his son to show how much he loves him. But how about us? Do we have the opportunity now to show that "Love is Spelled T-I-M-E" applies not only to children?

Remember the song, "Cat's in the Cradle"? It was a 1974 folk rock song by Harry Chapin. The lyrics were originally written as a poem by Chapin's wife, Sandy. The poem itself was inspired by the awkward relationship between Sandy's first husband and his father.

The song is told in first-person by a father who is too busy to spend time with his son. This continues throughout the son's youth, although he admires his father. In the song, the son says he will be just like his father when he grows up. Well, when the son grows up and the father is lonely and wants to see him and his family, the son is too busy. You see, he did grow up to be just like his father. It is a sad song, but, unfortunately, probably true for some families.

This story about the old man who thought he had wasted a day because he hadn't caught fish, whereas his son thought it was the best day of his life, has a powerful message. So does the song about the son not having time to spend with his lonely dad. The powerful message is: Love is spelled T-I-M-E. Think about having the time of your life again soon, and often.

Check out the correct spelling of the word "Love."

76

Improper Ending

Both written and spoken words are becoming too informal these days.

When someone asks me, "Where is he at?" I often respond with, "Don't you know you should never use a preposition to end a sentence with?" I do this in a kidding way with that silly kind of answer, but I really do mean it.

How's that for good advice? Does it really make a difference if words such as about, with, at, upon, after or except find their way to the end of a sentence? Does your appearance make a difference? Does your interaction with others make a difference? Does doing the right things in life make a difference? The answer is yes, they all make a difference.

An article titled "Good Manners, Good Grammar" in our local newspaper prompted several readers to comment. Some called to speak with me personally, and some sent e-mails. There seems to be a feeling that we are becoming too informal. This informality makes it easy for us to forget about our manners and about the quality of the written and spoken word. I think this is true—you see it every day.

What can we do about it? A number of things are possible. Here are a few suggestions:

- As parents and grandparents, we can set the right example by practicing good manners always and by using good grammar in writing and speaking.
- It is okay to correct family members if they use incorrect grammar. This can be done in a good-natured and friendly way.
- Make suggestions about improving manners, such as saying, "It would have been nice if you had stood when Mrs. Murphy came to our table."
- Communicate with your schoolteachers to encourage them to help with improved grammar. Thank them for all they do in this area.

- Give books and articles to friends and family members about good manners and good grammar.
- Share examples of common mistakes with children and grandchildren.

Additional examples were shared with me by readers of the "Good Manners, Good Grammar" article:

One reader said her pet peeve is people who cannot say "me" when they should in the objective case, such as after a preposition or as the object of a verb. They say, "They invited Roger and I to dinner," or "The matter is between Roger and I," even "This is Roger and I's house."

She continued with, "There is another thing—using "myself" instead of "me.""

I would like to add something to this "I, me and myself" subject. Some get confused about when to use "I," "me" or "myself." Here is a little discussion about these words that Gretchen and (I or me) would like to share with you. This also comes from some scholars and (I, me or myself).

The little test that we all remember, when deciding to use "I" or "me," is to eliminate the other part of the noun phrase to see how it sounds with each pronoun. In the example above, it would be, "Here is a little discussion about these words that **I** would like to share with you."

It seems that "myself" has crept into our usage because we sometimes don't like to use "me." A good rule to remember about myself is to use "myself" only when you have used "I" earlier in the same sentence. "I keep copies of *Sports Illustrated* magazines for myself."

All this confusion can easily be avoided if you just remove the second party from the sentences in which you feel tempted to use "myself" as an object or are not sure about "me." You wouldn't say, "This also comes from I" so you shouldn't say, "This also comes from some scholars and I." And you shouldn't say, "from some scholars and myself." The only correct way to say this is, "This also comes from some scholars and me."

Try to have fun with grammar.

Find a fun book on grammar from a local bookstore and give it to a child or grandchild. Spend time together sharing thoughts from the book.

77

CARING

Random Acts of Kindness

The family believes mother is rewarded for her kindness.

It is so important to provide little acts of kindness or random acts of kindness. The benefits and rewards are amazing. There are many, many examples of this every day. It's just a matter of awareness and appreciation to see them happening. I would like to share an example of acts of kindness from a couple in Iowa:

Chuck and Neva, along with a few other couples, were founders of a new Methodist Church in Des Moines. Chuck was chairman of the building committee, and through his connections, he arranged for Stanley Hess, a professor of art at Drake University, to design a brick and tile mural on the outside of the original sanctuary.

Chuck's company donated the glazed brick and Professor Hess donated the mural, which symbolized the Ascension of Christ, with the right hand raised in blessing and the left hand holding a cross made of Chi Rho, the first two letters of the New Testament word for Christ.

As far as is known, this was the first time that major features of a ceramic mural in Iowa were carved from unfired or "green" brick.

This was an act of kindness on the part of Professor Hess and Chuck that continues to be a visible reminder for all to see at Aldersgate Methodist Church.

Chuck and the building committee had a goal of building a perfect church. A problem developed during construction in that the cornerstone was flawed and cracked. Several others were burned at the same time and they were all cracked. A dedication ceremony was scheduled, which didn't allow time to replace the flawed cornerstone.

Chuck, the speaker at the dedication service, made a decision to use the imperfect stone. He said that since the church was imperfect and was for imperfect people, it was right to have an imperfect cornerstone. It was meant to be.

Some years later after Chuck died, his wife, Neva, purchased a life insurance policy with Aldersgate Methodist Church to be the beneficiary. Just last year, Neva decided how she wanted her insurance money to be spent. The sanctuary has a beautiful, round, stained glass window in the front of the sanctuary, but just plain glass windows around the side walls. Neva wanted to have these replaced with stained glass.

It was a wonderful idea, which she shared with her daughter and son. They were in agreement, but felt she should do it then. They wanted it to be done so that Neva could see the results of her contribution. She agreed. This was Neva's act of kindness for the church and the congregation.

Last week, Neva visited the church to see the new stained glass windows. She worried about this because she has macular degeneration and has difficulty seeing. She was afraid she wouldn't be able to see the windows. She had made up her mind, however, that she wasn't going to show disappointment if she couldn't see them. She didn't want to hurt the feelings of the contractor who had installed the windows.

When Neva walked into the church, she was amazed at how bright the entire sanctuary was. She could see clearly the stained glass windows. Neva was thrilled with how beautiful they looked and how much they added to the beauty of the original stained glass window. They all fit together in a spectacular way.

How did this happen? How could she see all this? The answer could be that this was God's act of kindness for Neva. He wanted her to see this beauty in His House.

I know this is a true story, because, you see, Chuck is my father and Neva is my mother.

Take time to share experiences of little acts of kindness with others.

78

CAREER

How Are You Doing?

Employees deserve to know how their work rates.

"How am I doing?" should be a positive question.

In another action, we discussed reasons why many workers and managers dread performance reviews. The reasons ranged from the reviewer not being adequately prepared to using a review system that is outdated or doesn't fit the situation.

There are many reasons why good performance reviews are important and should be something that both the reviewer and reviewee can look forward to:

- There is nothing more important at your company or organization than your employees. This should be the company's number-one asset.
- Employees deserve to know how they are doing and how they can improve their performance. It is a vital obligation of management to have this kind of communication.
- Time spent together with employees discussing how they are doing is valuable, exciting and an important part of every manager's job.

Positive actions to take

There are a number of things the reviewee can do to improve the performance review process, and in so doing, find out in greater detail how he or she is really doing. Along with this will be the benefit of knowing what is expected in the present job, areas to work on for performance improvement and what needs to be done for consideration for advancement.

The goal is to use the tools you have available to improve happiness and job satisfaction with improved communication regarding performance discussions. Two key tools are dedication and determination. If you are dedicated and determined to make this improvement happen, it will. Here are suggestions to make the review process more productive and something of value:

- Eliminate the negative aspects of performance reviews. There are answers and means to get around the negatives and move to the positives. As an example, schedule a discussion with your boss at mid-year ... with no mention of salary issues.
- Refer to your meeting as a discussion rather than a performance review. You should simply tell your boss you want to talk to him about how you are doing.
- Have a structure for this discussion, but don't be too structured. Have clearly in mind what you want to accomplish. Know your strengths and the areas in which you might need help.
- Listen very carefully to what your manager is saying during this meeting. Try to understand fully what he or she really means.
- Ask if your manager can help you to be more successful or to correct some shortcomings. Ask if there might be someone else in the company who could help.
- Ask the question, "What would you like to see me do differently?"
- It is okay to take notes during this discussion.
- If it is not clear what the manager is saying or referring to, ask for clarification. It is very important to have complete understanding during this discussion.
- Determine specific action items that you both agree should be done. Put these in writing, and have a time schedule for them.
- Be sure to thank your boss for his or her time, interest and comments.
- Don't let the meeting drag on too long. Since it probably will be in the office of the boss, it will be up to you to close the meeting. You will be the one leaving. Better to leave on your own than to be asked to leave.

Think about this. If you can have this kind of discussion with your manager about six months before your formal performance review, how much better your review will be. You will have known what to work on, and at your review, the earlier discussion will be fresh in both your mind and that of your manager

This is a good way to make the whole process much more positive and productive.

Share with your manager some special information about one of your good customers or about your industry.

79

CAREER

Lead, Don't Manage

Leading encourages positive, creative endeavors.

Is it time for you and your organization to move from the concept of being a manager to becoming a leader? One way to begin this process is to view your boss as your leader rather than your manager. The relationship between a leader and a follower is entirely different from that between a manager and employee.

This transition from manager to leader, as either the leader or follower, does not have to be a 50/50 kind of thing. If you want to make this happen, it is okay to do more than your share to start with. You know that is what a leader does naturally and automatically.

What is the difference and what changes need to take place to become a leader rather than a manager? I think the answers to these questions are quite simple. First of all, a leader leads his or her team to become more successful, happier and rewarded for their efforts.

A manager who is not a leader just manages things. There is a much different environment when a leader is leading. Leading encourages positive and creative endeavors. Leading provides the opportunity for the team to be the best it can be. In contrast, managing without leading results in the "8 to 5" kind of employee.

I saw a poster that impressed me with its wisdom and understanding of leadership. Look at what it says in just a few well-chosen words:

The Essence of Leadership

A true leader has the confidence to stand alone, the courage to make tough decisions, and the compassion to listen to the needs of others. He does not set out to be a leader, but becomes one by the quality of his actions and the integrity of his intent. In the end, leaders are much like eagles.... They don't flock, you find them one at a time.

I would add: "Leaders care, have the right priorities and take the actions that focus on caring and priorities."

A good manager is also a leader, but having the title of manager does not make the individual a leader. A manager can ask his employees to work for him and to follow his instruction, but he cannot ask his subordinates to follow him. "The Essence of Leadership" says the manager does not set out to be a leader, but becomes one by the quality of his actions and the integrity of his intent. You earn the right to be a leader. You earn this position of leadership by doing the right things.

I like to think of leadership as being a ten-letter word:

Listen	Listening
Evaluate	Evaluating what was said then
Act	Acting in an expedient way to make a
Difference	Difference for
Everyone	Everyone involved so that the
Right	Right things are done ensuring
Success	Success in an
Honest	Honest and
Intelligent	Intelligent way with
Patient	Patience and understanding for all

Using these ten letters can help in the transition from management to leadership. These thoughts can help to LEAD the way.

Today, treat your manager as if he or she were your leader.

80

A Good Leader = a Good Person

Traits may include compassion and trustworthiness.

There are many benefits for almost any individual or company when transitioning from manage to lead, manager to leader and finally from management to leadership. Leadership is a ten-letter word that begins with "L," which stands for being a good Listener and ends with "P" for being Patient. All the letters between "L" and "P" have equally important messages for those striving to become a good leader. The other eight letters were included in another action item.

You have seen many lists of traits or characteristics of a good manager. Some major companies have done extensive studies trying to identify which traits are most important for success. They use real people in the studies and then try to hire clones of these successful people. I don't think this works, because there are too many other factors that can't really be measured in a quantitative structure. There are also the timing factor and other outside influences that can't be measured in real time.

Perhaps finding a leader for your company or organization through promotion, an outside hire, or moving one from being a manager to becoming a leader is more of an art than a science. I think so, and that is why I would rather look at a fairly large list of traits of a good leader and see how well these fit the individual. Here is a list as an example:

Traits of a Good Leader

- Leads by example—walks the walk and talks the talk
- Is a good and compassionate listener
- Usually is a spiritual person
- Probably is a reader

- Thinks of others first
- Is a good communicator—always considers who needs to know and who thinks they need to know
- Communicates at the right level of difficulty to ensure understanding
- Knows where he or she is going and wants the team to share in the vision
- Is a winner and develops a winning team
- Is honest and can be trusted always—expects the same from the team
- Is not afraid to ask questions—it's okay to say "I don't know"
- Is one whom team members are proud to introduce as "my leader"
- Has a sense of humor—doesn't take himself or herself too seriously
- Is intelligent enough—willing to have more intelligent people on the team
- Is a quality person—attracts quality team members
- Is knowledgeable about the business
- Takes great joy in the success of the team members
- Makes opportunities available to employees—is a giver in the company
- Is an optimist
- Probably has a very happy home life—is successful in life as well as business
- Enjoys knowing about you and your family
- Is an opportunity-seeker—not a risk-avoider
- Has empathy and can put himself or herself in the other person's shoes. Can feel the pain
- Is a good guy or gal—know what this means? This is important
- Enjoys life and it shows

Doesn't it strike you that most of the traits of a good leader are the same as those of a good person? Interesting!

Share this list of traits of a good leader with someone whom you like and respect. Tell him or her that this list made you think of them.

81

Proper Introductions

Children learn good manners and grammar from their parents.

I have been surprised at the level of interest there is concerning manners and the use of proper grammar in our society today. Most people seem to be particularly bothered about the improper use of common words such as "me," "myself" and "I" in written or verbal communication.

What is interesting is that the comments are coming from people with good manners and good grammar. I'm not hearing much from the younger generation. Wonder why that is.

Parents set the tone for children to see how proper introductions should be made. It should be very natural to make introductions at the right time and in the right way. It should not be an awkward situation for either party.

Times have changed as far as the formality of proper introductions is concerned; I don't think this is a bad thing. I think introductions in the past were perhaps too formal and structured, resulting in uncomfortable feelings. This often led to not making introductions at all. There was the fear of not doing them correctly, so unfortunately, many introductions were missed.

As an example, "Mrs. Smith, may I present Mr. Jones." This is proper in a formal social setting where the man is introduced to the woman. Another rule we learned is that the less important person should be introduced to the more important person. Also a younger person should be introduced to an older person.

All this adds to the confusion. Who is more important? What about introducing a younger person to an older person if the younger person is a woman and the older person is a man? Can you always tell who is older?

What also has changed is that there is no such thing as gender in the business world. It is rank that counts when making an introduction, not gender at all. And in the business world, all should shake hands during introductions, whereas in social settings, women may or may not shake hands. The same is true regarding rising when being introduced. In business, women should also rise when they are introduced.

So, what is important today in making introductions?

- Take the time and effort to make them. This is the most important.
- Include everyone when making introductions.
- If you shake hands with some in a group, shake hands with everyone.
- It is good to repeat the name of the person you are meeting. It is a nice touch and it's helpful in remembering the person's name.
- Tell a little something about the person being introduced. This will make it easier for a dialog to start between the people being introduced.
- If you forget someone's name, ask them to repeat it, or introduce yourself; the other person probably will say his or her name. You also can simply say, "I have forgotten your name; I'm sorry."

I don't think you should make a big deal out of the structure of the introduction. Instead make a big deal out of introducing people who don't know each other. It is the person who counts, not who is mentioned first.

Take the opportunity to introduce yourself to someone you have wanted to meet.

82

Look Up, Young Man, Look Up

Optimists look up, while pessimists look down.

Look up, young man, look up—or was the well-known saying, "Go West, Young Man, Go West," by Horace Greeley?

Actually, Horace Greeley was incorrectly credited with this famous quote, which was originally written by John B. L. Soule in 1851. Along with being wrongly credited to Mr. Greeley, it has often been misquoted. It was originally written as, "Go West, young man, and grow up with the country."

I think today Greeley or Soule would say, "Look up young people, look up."

At the beginning of each day and many times during the day, we can choose to look down, look straight ahead or look up. What does this mean? It can mean many things, but I think it has to do with choices we make for ourselves and our lives on a daily basis.

It could mean that we are living in the past, which would be looking down. Or it could be living for today, which would refer to looking straight ahead. And it could be living for the future, which would be looking up.

It could also refer to being optimistic or pessimistic about life. Looking down would be pessimistic and looking up would be positive and optimistic. Looking straight ahead perhaps is neither pessimistic nor optimistic; it is just living life—maybe in a set routine and drifting from day to day without focus on priorities.

It could also refer to a relationship with God. Looking down would seem to say that God is not a part of everyday life. Looking straight ahead could mean believing in God but not growing in Christian faith. Looking up could mean having a strong relationship with God and listening to Him.

Appreciation for the past is important because "Those who ignore history are doomed to repeat it." Appreciation for the past and the study of history are different from living in the past. Living in the past is looking down, while studying history would be looking ahead or looking up or both.

Living for today is looking straight ahead and also looking up if today is being lived in the right way. "This is the day the Lord has made/We will rejoice and be glad in it."

Looking up seems to signify all that is good and positive in life. It is hope, faith, optimism and confidence in today and tomorrow.

Have you actually thought much about the word UP? This two-letter word perhaps has more meanings than any other.

It's easy to understand UP, meaning toward the sky or at the top of the list, but when we awaken in the morning, why do we wake UP?

At a meeting, why does a topic come UP? Why do we speak UP? Why are officers UP for election? Why is it UP to the secretary to write UP the report?

We call UP our friends, and we refer to brightening UP a room and polishing UP the silver; we warm UP leftovers and clean UP the kitchen.

We lock UP the house and some guys fix UP the old car. At other times, the little word has very special meaning. People stir UP trouble, line UP for tickets, work UP an appetite and think UP excuses. To be dressed is one thing, but to be dressed UP is special.

This UP is confusing: A drain must be opened UP because it is stopped UP. We open UP a store in the morning but we close it UP at night. We seem to be pretty mixed UP about UP.

In a dictionary, UP takes UP almost one-fourth of the page and can add UP to about thirty definitions. If you are UP to it, you might try building UP a list of the many ways UP is used. It will take UP a lot of your time, but if you don't give UP, you may wind UP with a hundred or more. When it threatens to rain, we say it is clouding UP. When the sun comes out, we say it is clearing UP.

When it rains, it wets the earth and often messes things UP. When it doesn't rain for a while, things dry UP. One could go on and on, but I'll wrap it UP, for now my time is UP.

So ... it is time to shut UP.

You're the one to choose to look down, look straight ahead or to look up.... It's UP to you.

Look UP an old friend and spend some quality time together making UP for lost time.

83

CULTIVATE CHARACTER

Don't Take Yourself Too Seriously

Real leaders have a good sense of humor.

An individual told me how much she enjoys satire. She went on to add that she has laughter all day long. Even when she is alone, she still has laughter. She knows where to go to find it. Isn't that great?

Having laughter all day and enjoying all kinds of humor is good for your health and happiness. No doubt about it. A travel agent some years ago gave us some advice before going on a cruise. He said that while traveling abroad or taking cruises, something was bound to go wrong. You can expect it and when it happens, he advised us, just step back and look at the experience as amusing. You know, it really does work. Try it sometime. Just say to yourself and those with whom you are traveling, "This really is amusing." And then laugh about it.

It is fun to think about humor. There are many places to find it. I like to read about Benjamin Franklin and have found his humor to be ageless. Benjamin Franklin was a real master at so many things. He was a great leader who accomplished so much in his lifetime. What an example he is for us to study and enjoy.

Benjamin Franklin showed that a real leader has a good sense of humor and the ability to lead without taking himself or herself too seriously. I am reminded of a description I read about what makes a leader: intelligence, passion, strength, devotion, charisma, tenacity, perseverance, generosity and forgiveness. I would add a good sense of humor, as well.

Benjamin Franklin possessed all of these qualities, including a good sense of humor; that is why he is considered to be one of the greatest American minds. His life is truly the "American Dream." Few people would have surmised that Franklin, the son of a candlemaker, would master so many disciplines. His story proves that with determination and dedication, success is within anyone's grasp.

Franklin developed a satirical style of writing that examined the political, personal, and social issues of the time. Whether he was poking fun at conservative Bostonians or laughing at the battle of the sexes, Franklin's style was entertaining, while carrying a message. His satirical pieces "made 'em laugh," but also "made 'em think."

Benjamin Franklin's quotations are famous, and I think many are as timely today as they were years ago. A few examples follow:

- *Well done is better than well said.*
- *Think of these things, whence you came, where you are going, and to whom you must account.*
- *The sleeping fox catches no poultry.*
- *Never leave till tomorrow that which you can do today.*
- *Little strokes fell great oaks.*
- *If you would persuade, you must appeal to interest rather than intellect.*
- *Hide not your talents. They for use were made. What's a sundial in the shade?*
- *He that goes a borrowing goes a sorrowing.*
- *A little neglect may breed mischief ... for want of a nail, the shoe was lost; for want of a shoe the horse was lost; and for want of a horse the rider was lost.*
- *Early to bed, early to rise makes a man healthy, wealthy, and wise.*
- *God helps them that help themselves.*
- *Haste makes waste.*
- *There never was a good war nor a bad peace.*
- *They that can give up essential liberty to obtain a little temporary safety deserve neither liberty nor safety.*

Don't you just love these old quotations from Franklin? They really do make you think. Consider our political situation today. An example: "If you would persuade, you must appeal to interest rather than intellect." This would be a good message for many politicians.

How about, "They that can give up essential liberty to obtain a little temporary safety deserve neither liberty nor safety." This would be for those politicians who think the war on terror is a bumper sticker.

I would think Franklin would want us to have laughter in our lives every day and not to take ourselves too seriously.

Share a good joke or a funny story with someone close to you today. Make someone laugh—and you too.

84

Finding a Job Can Be Work

Decide if the time is right.

The economy is not doing very well. Interest rates are low, but inflation probably will be a problem soon; unemployment is as high as it's been in a long time.

Many have lost a great deal in the stock market and there are so many uncertainties now that it is hard to do any long-term planning. With all these negative indicators, you would think this would not be a good time to be job-hunting.

Well it is and it isn't. It really depends on the individual and his or her attitude and desire regarding finding the right job. If you have a friend who is without a job or is considering changing jobs, you might tell him or her about the following suggestions:

Suggestion Number One: Do an analysis of your situation.

If you have been fired, terminated or your job has been eliminated, the first suggestion is to do an analysis to determine what really happened. If the economy has forced your company to cut back employment, this could perhaps be your analysis. If you are questioning why you were affected and others were not, however, go ahead with the analysis.

Because there is the threat of lawsuits, companies are cautious about giving you the real reasons for your termination, or at least all of the reasons. Giving too much information could open the door for the employee to present objections that might be valid. This means it is up to you to do the investigative work to put all the pieces together.

Start with the assumption that companies do not want to terminate employees. They would much rather keep an employee who is doing his or her job than take the time and money to search for a replacement. So, when someone is terminated or demoted, it probably is something that was done after a great deal of thought and serious discussions with others in the company.

If you aren't sure about what happened or why, consider visiting with some friends at your old company whom you would trust and who you think would be honest with you. You want this information so that you can do things differently at your next job.

It is okay to share this with your friends. Let them know you want the information for the right reasons. You want to learn from this information, not to use it in preparing for a lawsuit.

Suggestion Number Two: Do an honest self-analysis.

This suggestion is for those who have been terminated and for those who are unhappy with their present job.

Suggestion number-two is to do an in-depth self-analysis of your strengths, weaknesses, experience, and probably most important of all, what you are good at and like doing. Take the time to compile four lists: Strengths, Weaknesses, Experience, and Enjoy Doing.

If you have been terminated, you have been given a wonderful opportunity to take the time to do this self-analysis. If you are employed, it is difficult to have time and the right motivation to make the analysis. Finding a job is a job, and if you are still employed, it is hard to take time for self-analysis and job-hunting. Think of a job search as full-time employment if you are serious about finding a new or different job.

Suggestion Number Three: Develop a plan of action.

Use all the information you compiled and learned from suggestions number-one and number-two to help develop a plan of action. This will be the basis for determining what kind of job you will seek, contacts and networking, information to include in your résumé and what to highlight in your cover letter.

The purpose for using these three suggestions is to help you identify the right job for you, considering your strengths, interests and experience. Another action included in this book is "Plan the Work and Work the Plan." This action is to help with the next step in finding the right job.

Focus on communication at your job. Many terminations ultimately are due to a breakdown in communication concerning expectations.

85

CULTIVATE CHARACTER

A Good Manager Must Be a Good Leader, Too

You can depend on it.

A few years ago, I was giving a talk on leadership to a group of employees at a company in Chicago. The main message was that it is far better to lead than manage and more effective to be a leader than a manager. Focusing on leadership skills instead of management skills was the purpose of the meeting.

We discussed many traits of a good leader. Here are a few of my favorites:

- Leads by example—walks the walk and talks the talk
- Is a good and compassionate listener
- Is a good communicator—considers always who needs to know and who thinks they need to know. Communicates at the right level of difficulty to ensure understanding
- Is a winner and develops a winning team
- Is honest and can be trusted always—expects the same from the team
- Is an optimist
- Is a quality person—attracts quality team members
- Has a sense of humor—doesn't take himself or herself too seriously
- Is intelligent enough—willing to have more intelligent people on the team

Toward the end of the meeting, one of the participants in the class said the biggest problem she had was with her manager, who was not dependable. A number of others agreed that they had the same problem. They just couldn't depend on their managers to give them the answers they needed or provide information necessary to complete their assignments. Many felt they were being held up by undependable managers.

When I was a boy in Des Moines, Iowa, I had a summer job as a bricklayer's helper. My job was to keep the bricklayers supplied with bricks and mortar. The owner of this masonry contracting company explained the job to me by saying, "The bricklayer is a dollar bill and you, the helper, are a nickel." He added that he never wanted to see the dollar bill waiting for the nickel. I understood. The message was very clear.

I wonder today, with everyone in business so busy, if sometimes managers forget that they might be holding up nickels that are holding up dollars by not being dependable.

You know, being dependable is just so basic that you would not even think about putting it on a list of traits of good leaders. But when you think about it, how often do you need to follow up with certain people? Some always return telephone calls on time and some don't. Not returning a telephone call not only is being undependable—it is inconsiderate.

It is a good exercise every now and then to do a personal evaluation of yourself and your job. This should include the following questions: Am I dependable? Can my team or my manager always depend on me to do my job and get my assignments completed when they are due? Do I ALWAYS return my telephone calls on time? Am I being questioned about the status of my projects or assignments earlier than I should be? Is there a message there?

How often do you use or hear the word "dependable" in describing a friend or co-worker? It would be a nice compliment.

Compliment someone today on being a dependable friend or a dependable employee.

We Should All Listen to Lombardi

"Winning isn't everything; it's the only thing."

Vince Lombardi is well known for his famous sayings about football and winning. It was Lombardi who said, "If it doesn't matter who wins or loses, then why do they keep score?" He also said, "If winning isn't everything, why do they keep score?"

Many coaches, managers and presidents of ball clubs and even companies quote Lombardi's two favorite sayings: "Winning is not everything, but wanting to win is." This is followed by, "Winning isn't everything; it's the only thing."

Let's say a large university in the United States, which has a long tradition of having a winning football program, hires a new president. This new president has never played football and doesn't really know much about the game. He has a great educational background, has gone to all the right schools and has excelled in academics. Because he is also a great speaker, he easily impressed the university's board of regents and the search committee.

This new president was hired with a great deal of fanfare, but without anyone's knowing what he thought about the football program, its importance to the school and the alumni support. The campus newspaper knew how the president felt, but they didn't like football either, so it wasn't reported. It turns out that this president had some ideas of his own about what is right for the school, the conference and football in general.

First of all, a few people from the other schools in their conference had complained that the new president's school was able to attract better athletes and offer more scholarships. He agreed that this wasn't really fair, so he developed a new policy regarding scholarships and which athletes to go after.

His fairness plan was for all of their athletes to give half of their scholarship money to a general fund that would go to the poorer schools. In addition, he decreed that the top athletes would not be offered scholarships at their school. In doing this, the athletes would be encouraged or forced to go to the other schools. This would help balance the talent level.

Some of the coaches complained that the school consistently tackled hard and tried to force fumbles. They also said the secondary was always trying to knock the ball loose after the other team made a reception. The president agreed with them that it just wasn't fair the way the defense was playing. The president told the coach that there would be no more trying to force fumbles, and if a fumble occurred, his ballplayers would not try to recover it. They also would do only arm-tackling in the future.

There was also criticism that his school's offense was too wide open, and it was difficult to defend against this kind of offense. It just wasn't fair. The president agreed and promised that the team would only run one-direction plays on first and second downs and only pass on third down—then only if they needed more than eight yards. This way the defense could do a better job of holding down the scoring.

The other schools complained that his school had scouts who were scouting their games; they didn't think this was the right thing to do. The president said they would do no more scouting in the future. Their scouts, however, were welcome to come to any of his school's games. That would help them like his school and team more. In fact, to make them like the school even more, the president would provide them with their game plan before the game. Now, how is that for winning friends and influencing people?

The president apologized for all the things the past president and his coach had done to have a winning team. He is promoting change at the school so that all schools would be able to share the success and problems in a more equitable way.

Lombardi, I'm sure, is asking, "Could something like this ever happen?" I'm also quite sure that Lombardi is saying, "Winning the war on terror isn't everything; it is the only thing."

Listen to Lombardi!

Contact your congressman and tell him to "listen to Lombardi."

87

Who Says Spaghetti Doesn't Grow on Trees?

It's not hard to be an April Fool.

Over the years our family, like many others, has looked forward to fooling family members on April Fools' Day. Most of the time the tricks don't work, but we keep trying.

As the years go on, it gets harder and harder to fool each other. Even if the ideas are clever, everyone on April 1 is expecting a call or is on the lookout for something to happen. There have been some really good ones that we like to remember and talk about, especially after the current trick hasn't worked. Again this year, no one in our family was fooled, but that doesn't mean we won't try again next year.

There probably were memorable tricks played on you and by you. It's fun to remember them. Did you ever think about writing them down so they could be remembered and shared in the future?

I read an article listing the top 100 April Fool's Day hoaxes of all time. It led me to investigate how April Fools' Day came to be; I found that the origin is obscure. One likely theory is that the modern holiday was first celebrated soon after the adoption of the Gregorian calendar. The term April Fool referred to someone still adhering to the Julian calendar, which it replaced.

In many pre-Christian cultures, May Day (May 1) was celebrated as the first day of summer and signaled the start of the spring planting season. An April Fool may have been someone who did this prematurely.

Did you know that in some countries, such as the UK, Australia, New Zealand, Canada and South Africa, the April Fools' jokes or tricks only last until noon? One who plays a trick after noon is called an April Fool. Elsewhere, such as in Ireland, France and America, the jokes last all day.

You may think your own tricks or hoaxes were great, but how do they compare with this list of a few of the top 100 April Fools' Day hoaxes of all time?

1. The Swiss Spaghetti Harvest: In 1957 a respected BBC show announced that, thanks to a very mild winter and the virtual elimination of the dreaded spaghetti weevil, Swiss farmers were enjoying a bumper spaghetti crop. Swiss peasants were shown pulling strands of spaghetti down from trees. Huge numbers of viewers were taken in.

2. Sidd Finch: In 1985 *Sports Illustrated* published a story about a new rookie pitcher who planned to play for the Mets. It was reported that he threw a baseball at 168 mph with pinpoint accuracy. Surprisingly, Sidd Finch had never even played the game. Instead, he had mastered the "art of the pitch" in a Tibetan monastery. Mets fans celebrated their team's amazing luck at having found such a gifted player until they found out he existed only in the imagination of the author of the article, George Plimpton.

3. Instant Color TV: In 1962 there was only one TV channel in Sweden and it broadcast in black and white. The station's technical expert appeared on the news to announce that, thanks to new technology, viewers could convert their existing sets to display color reception. All they had to do was pull a nylon stocking over their TV screens. Thousands of people were taken in.

4. The Taco Liberty Bell: In 1996 the Taco Bell Corporation announced it had bought the Liberty Bell and was renaming it the Taco Liberty Bell. Hundreds of outraged citizens called the National Historic Park in Philadelphia to express their anger. Their nerves were calmed only when Taco Bell revealed, a few hours later, that it was all a practical joke.

5. The Left-Handed Whopper: In 1998 Burger King published a full-page advertisement in *USA Today* announcing the introduction of a new item to their menu: a Left-Handed Whopper, specially designed for the 32 million Americans who are left-handed. The following day Burger King issued a release revealing that although the Left-Handed Whopper was a hoax, thousands of customers had gone into their restaurants to request the new sandwich. Simultaneously, according to the press release, many others requested their own right-handed version.

Well, take your time between now and April 1 to work on your trick, which might be even better than these five.

Consider doing April Fools' tricks at other times of the year.

88

CELEBRATING

Priorities, Priorities, Priorities

There are many ways to stay focused on priorities.

I have been asked why I wrote my first book, *Time Out ... It's Your Call.* Although there were a number of reasons, I feel comfortable talking about one that prompted me to begin writing the book.

Before I retired from ABB, a large international electrical manufacturer, I felt if I could take all I had learned and experienced during my career and go back twenty or thirty years, how valuable that would be. That, of course was not possible, so I decided to put those experiences and the many lessons learned in writing. That way they could be shared with family, friends and others.

Another reason was that I wanted to share the priorities and actions described in the book, because I feel focusing on the right priorities in life is so important. There was also a very strong religious motivation in writing the book.

I think it is important to have reminders in life that bring us back to focusing on our priorities. Let me share with you *A Thousand Marbles,* by Jeffrey Davis, a motivational story about priorities in life. The protagonist tells of listening on his ham radio to a conversation between two other men.

"I turned the dial up into the phone portion of the band on my ham radio in order to listen to a Saturday morning swap net. Along the way, I came across an older-sounding chap with a tremendous signal and a golden voice. You know the kind—he sounded as though he should be in the broadcasting business. He was telling whomever he was talking with something about a thousand marbles. I was intrigued and stopped to listen to what he had to say."

Well, Tom, it sure sounds like you're busy with your job. I'm sure they pay you well but it's a shame you have to be away from home and your family so much. Hard to believe a young fellow should have to work sixty or seventy hours a week to make ends meet. Too bad you missed your daughter's dance recital.

Let me tell you something, Tom—something that has helped me keep a good perspective on my own priorities.

"And that's when he began to explain his theory of a thousand marbles."

You see, I sat down one day and did a little arithmetic. The average person lives about seventy-five years. I know, some live more and some live less, but on average, folks live about seventy-five years.

Now, then, I multiplied 75 times 52 and I came up with 3,900, which is the number of Saturdays that the average person has in their entire lifetime. Now, stick with me Tom, I'm getting to the important part.

It took me until I was fifty-five years old to think about all this in any detail, and by that time, I had lived through over twenty-eight hundred Saturdays. I got to thinking that if I lived to be seventy-five, I only had about a thousand of them left to enjoy.

So I went to a toy store and bought every single marble they had. I ended up having to visit three toy stores to round up 1,000 marbles. I took them home and put them inside a large, clear plastic container right here in the shack next to my gear.

Every Saturday since then, I have taken one marble out and thrown it away. I found that by watching the marbles diminish, I focused more on the really important things in life. There is nothing like watching your time here on this earth run out to help get your priorities straight.

Now, let me tell you one last thing before I sign off with you and take my lovely wife out for breakfast. This morning, I took the very last marble out of the container. I figure if I make it until next Saturday, then I have been given a little extra time. And the one thing we can all use is a little more time.

It was nice to meet you, Tom. I hope you spend more time with your family, and I hope to meet you again here on the band. 73 Old Man, this is K9NZQ, clear and going QRT, good morning!

"You could have heard a pin drop on the band when this fellow signed off. I guess he gave us all a lot to think about.

"I had planned to work on the antenna that morning, and then I was going to meet up with a few hams to work on the next club newsletter.

"Instead, I went upstairs and woke my wife up with a kiss. 'C'mon, honey, I'm taking you and the kids to breakfast.'

'What brought this on?' she asked with a smile.

'Oh, nothing special; it's just been a long time since we spent a Saturday together with the kids. Hey, can we stop at a toy store while we're out? I need to buy some marbles.'"

It's not difficult to calculate how many marbles you'll need to purchase. Why not start your own marble container? Did this story move you? Did it move you enough to consider making some changes in your life to focus on your most important priorities? I'll bet it did.

Develop a visible method to remind yourself how important it is to focus on your priorities. Maybe it's marbles.

89

CELEBRATING

It's the Most Wonderful Time of the Year

"For everything there is a season...."

It's the most wonderful time of the year
With the kids jingle belling and everyone telling you
'Be of good cheer'
It's the most wonderful time of the year.

It's the hap - happiest season of all
With those holiday greetings and gay, happy meetings
When friends come to call,
it's the hap - happiest season of all.

For many, Christmas time is the most wonderful time of the year. For others, it is Thanksgiving time with family and friends. For some, it might be summer vacations together or skiing in the mountains during spring break. Or it might be celebrating birthdays and anniversaries. Perhaps all are wonderful times of the year if we want them to be.

This is a wonderful time of the year to think about our favorite times—a time to give thanks; a time for anticipation of the New Year fast approaching.

It is written in Ecclesiastes 3, "For everything there is a season, and a time for every matter under heaven." There are 14 "a time to" statements that follow 3.1. They are all important, but two seem to speak to me at this time of the year. "A time to keep, and a time to throw away"; "A time to keep silence, and a time to speak."

To me this is saying to think about the year and keep those good memories and thoughts with you and throw away negative feelings. It also is saying it is a time to keep silent about unpleasant things that happened to you during the year and a time to speak out to say to others, "thanks" or "I'm sorry."

It is a time to really think about time. What is time? Think about it. How often do you hear that time just flew by? Time is time; it doesn't go faster or slower. It's how we use time that makes it seem to be variable.

"I had the best time." "I really had a bad time." I don't really think it is the time that was good or bad; it was how we spent the time that was either good or bad. There is some kind of lesson to be learned thinking about time. We know we only have so much time each day and only so much time in every lifetime. So, isn't it up to us to decide how we want to spend our time?

This might be the right time of year to be thinking about next year and how you plan to spend your time. Some of this planning might be about New Year's resolutions and some might be about having more of "the most wonderful time of the year" times.

A suggestion might be to include some "my time" in each day. Ideally, it would be at a regular time of day in a regular place that is quiet and conducive to just thinking or praying or both.

Another suggestion would be to think seriously about priorities in life. Spending time on high priorities would definitely add to the opportunity for creating more "wonderful times."

A third suggestion would be to commit to time management in your everyday life. Separate tasks to be done into A, B and C classifications; tackle the A items before doing the B, and then deal with the C items. It is very worthwhile to do first things first.

Another suggestion would be to make sure you take time to have plenty of "fun" times.

It's time to wish you all the best for a wonderful holiday season and a wonderful new year.

Make this a wonderful time of the year for you and your family.

90

CARING

Be Prepared

If an apology is in order, do it right.

If there is a need for making an apology, we have much to learn from Randy Pausch, who was a professor at Carnegie Mellon University. You probably remember Randy, who shared some thoughts about success during his "Last Lecture."

Randy learned that he was dying of cancer and used this last lecture to talk about living, not dying. He told about a few of the guiding principles in his life. One was to tell the truth always. Another was to apologize when you have done something wrong.

Randy said a good apology has three important parts: I'm sorry; It's my fault; How do I make it right? He said most people forget the last part—How do I make it right?.

Making an apology for something you did that was wrong should not be taken lightly. It should not be done without thoughtful planning. Here are some ideas about "planning the work (apology) and working the plan":

- Be positive and optimistic. Plan to be successful!
- Be sure you fully understand what you did that was wrong and assess how badly the person was hurt.
- An apology is not the time to be making excuses or to share the blame with anyone else. It is you who are making the apology.
- Put yourself in the other person's position. What would you expect the person to say to you with the apology? How would you receive the apology?
- Take the time to put your apology in writing. This will help you to get your thoughts straight and can be given to the person after the apology. Don't you think giving a written apology to the person you hurt will help to show that you really mean what you are saying? It will also give him or her something to take along and think about after your verbal apology. Maybe the individual will respond in writing with a letter of forgiveness.

- Mean what you say and say what you mean. Be sincere. If this is not possible for you at this time, wait until the time is right to make the apology. A good late apology is better than a poor, quick one. Not too late, however.
- Ask what you can do to make it right. Do you have some suggestions that you might offer if the person doesn't have any ideas for you to make amends?
- If there is something that you agree should be done, make sure you do it when you said you would; try to do more than what was promised.
- Make your apology in the right environment. You should be alone with the person receiving the apology and you should make sure you have adequate time to spend together. It would be a mistake to rush off to a meeting when you are having a good sharing time together.
- There is no reason to ask if the person is mad or still mad at you. This could just start the whole thing over again and, yes, he or she probably is still mad, but in time will get over it.
- Be kind and patient. You may not get the response you want in the first meeting with the first apology. That is okay, so just leave the door open for reconciliation at some later date.
- If the apology has been accepted and you believe the time is right, go ahead and ask for forgiveness.
- Don't prolong the apology or rehash what has happened. Conclude the meeting with a positive, upbeat plan to do something fun together in the near future.

If there is someone in the past to whom you should have said "I'm sorry," get prepared and do it now.

91

Just Do Something

Go back to the basics.

We had a football coach in high school who was quite a guy. His name was Archie Johnson, and I miss him a lot. I wish I could just see him again to tell him how much I appreciated all he did for our school, for me and for all the other Des Moines Roosevelt High School athletes.

He was a very good coach, who taught us more than we realized at the time. He would say things that just plain made sense and you would remember them. An example of this was yelling "just do something." In other words, don't stand around and get in the way of others. Tackle your own man if you have to, but do something.

He also had a way of showing he wasn't happy with what we did. If I missed a block or a tackle, he would say, "nice block" or "nice tackle, Jan." Jan was my sister and I knew exactly what he meant—he didn't mix up our names.

Archie also told us, coached us and made us believe that we didn't have to be the biggest to win games. One on one, he showed us how it was more important to be in the right position with the right leverage to block someone bigger, and the same with making a clean tackle. He was also one to lecture us that if we planned to win and really believed it, it would happen.

He loved basics and we had plenty of basics on those hot, two-a-day practices in August. He was right to stress the importance of mastering the basics. His abilities were recognized statewide as he was voted Iowa High School Coach of the Year our senior year.

Archie was a man of strong character, doing what he loved for the right reasons. He loved football and he loved working with the kids. That is why he was a high school football coach. I know he was a man who felt his integrity, honesty and loyalty were extremely important. I know he believed there was no amount of money that would be worth compromising his integrity, honesty or loyalty. There are lots and lots of people like that in our country. Unfortunately, there are others who for money or personal publicity or to get even, will compromise all three—integrity, honesty and loyalty.

Some write books that are critical of our leaders, our administration, our government and our country. Generally, these are politically motivated; the writer must think that the end justifies the means. Why in the world would anyone give ammunition to our enemies and those around the world who hate us? Is there enough money to justify doing this? Apparently some think there is.

With many of these books, it appears that much is untrue or at least exaggerated; many times there are just opinions, not facts. But the question is that even if what they are writing is true, why would they do such a thing? You don't go to the opposing football team's coaches and tell them your quarterback is a weak passer under pressure and can't throw on the run. What kind of loyalty would that be to your school or your team?

What kind of loyalty is it to our country to be writing negative things about our leaders and our government? I think it shows a complete lack of character; it clearly shows that the writer and his or her publisher are willing to sell out their integrity, honesty and loyalty for bad, bad reasons.

I just wish we could have these negative writers join Archie and his old players in Iowa for two-a-day drills in August this year. Archie could teach them the important basics in life and the ballplayers could physically show them how the team feels about their actions. How much fun would that be?

 Don't buy books that are politically motivated to be negative about the United States of America and our leaders. Speak up—just do something!

92

Seventeen Words

What has made you successful?

Almost every day we find ourselves in a position in which we have to make decisions and solve problems. This happens in both our business and personal lives. Normally, solving a problem or making a difficult decision is not something we were planning to do. We are already doing other things, have other plans and want to finish those tasks that are in front of us.

Generally speaking, we really don't have a choice. The problem is a problem and it has to be solved. The decision that has to be made most often has a time frame that demands our immediate attention. The problem and the need for making a decision won't just go away. So it is safe to say that decision-making and problem-solving are high priorities in our lives, and we have to accept the responsibility to deal with them.

If you were asked at your retirement party to describe what had made you successful, what would you say? There are many good answers, such as working with good people, good bosses, favorable market conditions, competitive products and so forth. These might all be true, but I'll wager that having the ability to make good decisions and solve problems might be the most important contributor to your success.

Some truly believe that problems create opportunities. Taking good care of a customer who has a problem is a way to demonstrate the strong character of your company and your people. It is worth giving the customer more than he asks for when handling a complaint. If the customer asks for bread, give him cake. The customer will be impressed and you will be rewarded for turning the problem into an opportunity.

When faced with a decision to make, or a problem to solve, take the time to make sure the facts are known and the possible alternatives are considered. After this is done, try taking some time to let your subconscious mind work on the problem or the decision. I think you will be amazed at what happens if you let your mind do its job.

I read about a successful executive who said at his retirement party, "Let me tell you why I've enjoyed such success. Years ago I had a great boss and mentor. One day he gave me his business card. On the back, he'd written seventeen words. He told me that whenever he had a tough decision to make, or a problem to solve, he'd read each of these words. Then he'd close his eyes, pray, and be quiet. Each time he did, something amazing would happen: one of the words would jump out at him and steer him in the right direction. These seventeen words never failed him and have never failed me."

The seventeen words:

PREPARE ... LISTEN ... SMILE ... LOVE ... CHOOSE ... FOCUS ... BELIEVE ... RELAX ... ACT ... FORGIVE ... PRAY ... TRUST ... CHANGE ... PERSIST ... ACCEPT ... RISK ... WAIT

I would like to recommend that these ideas be used together. The first is to collect all the facts and information about the problem or decision to be made. Then give your subconscious mind some time to work on the problem—perhaps overnight. After that, slowly and thoughtfully read all seventeen words. Follow this by closing your eyes, praying and being quiet. See if one or more of these words jump out at you.

Is it time to be thinking about what you would say at your retirement party? If you are retired, what advice would you like to give to someone you care about who is still working?

Believe that problems can create opportunities if handled in the right way.

93

CELEBRATING

A Time for Thanks

Remember all those patriotic quotes.

Each year we look forward to a long July 4th weekend. During this fun time of fireworks, cookouts, good times with family and friends and flying the American flag, we should take the opportunity to say thanks to our founding fathers who made this all possible. Will we remember to give thanks to those who are today fighting for our freedom so that we can have these good times on July 4th?

I think it is appropriate to celebrate Independence Day and to picture what it must have been like back in 1776. Imagine what great foresight and courage it took to take this stand against Great Britain.

The United States Declaration of Independence is an act of the Second Continental Congress, adopted on July 4, 1776, which declared that the Thirteen Colonies in North America were "Free and Independent States" and that "all political connection between them and the State of Great Britain, is and ought to be totally dissolved."

The Declaration is considered to be the founding document of the United Sates of America, where July 4 is celebrated as Independence Day and the nation's birthday. It is interesting to note that John Hancock, as the elected President of Congress, was the only person to sign the Declaration of Independence on July 4. It was not until the following month on August 2 that the remaining 55 other delegates began to sign the document.

Edward Rutledge (age 26) was the youngest signer, and Benjamin Franklin (age 70) was the oldest.

In a remarkable series of coincidences, both John Adams and Thomas Jefferson, two founding fathers of the U.S. and the only two men who signed the Declaration of Independence to become President of the United States, died on the same day: July 4, 1826, which was the United States' 50th anniversary. President James Monroe died exactly five years later on July 4, 1831, though he did not sign the Declaration of Independence.

Since our birthday on July 4, 1776, there have been many patriotic quotes speaking of our freedom and our form of government. I wish all Americans, especially our politicians, would reflect on what our founding fathers did for us. I also wish that some of these famous patriotic quotations would come to life again:

A patriot must always be ready to defend his country against his government.
Edward Abbey

Democracy is the government of the people, by the people, for the people.
Abraham Lincoln

He loves his country best who strives to make it best. Robert Green Ingersoll

In the truest sense, freedom cannot be bestowed; it must be achieved.
Franklin D. Roosevelt

It is easy to take liberty for granted, when you have never had it taken from you.
Dick Cheney

Loyalty to the country always. Loyalty to the government when it deserves it.
Mark Twain

Then join hand in hand, brave Americans all! By uniting we stand, by dividing we fall.
John Dickinson

We must learn to live together as brothers or perish together as fools.
Martin Luther King Jr.

We can give thanks to our founding fathers and our servicemen and women when celebrating the birthday of our country, but most important is to thank God that we are Americans.

When you see people in uniform, thank them for all they are doing for our country.

94

CULTIVATE CHARACTER

Focus on Listening

We're often too busy to spare even a few minutes.

How often do you spend time listening to yourself? You know you have some very valuable thoughts that should be shared—shared with you.

Why is it that we don't listen to ourselves? I think one reason is that we are too busy. We get into a routine that is fast-paced, without spare time to meditate and think about life. Unfortunately, all too often this also applies to taking time to pray.

I think another reason we don't listen to ourselves is that we really don't want to hear what we have to say. It's hard not to be honest with ourselves, so sometimes we choose not to listen.

> *This above all: to thine own self be true. And it must follow, as the night the day, Thou canst not then be true to any man.* William Shakespeare

Let's take time today to focus on listening. The following are some insights into the fine art of being a good listener:

- Knowledge is talking less and being a good listener.
- Love is listening to what is really being said and meant, not only the words.
- Listen for the real meaning and try to understand what is being said and why.
- Listen to everyone who speaks to you. Don't be a selective listener.
- Concentrate on what the speaker is saying. Try to avoid thinking about what you are going to say until the speaker has stopped talking. Think about this.
- Think about waiting for a count of 3 to 5 after someone has stopped talking before you say anything. That way you are sure not to interrupt them.
- Listening is learning. It's hard to learn when you are talking.

- If you are not completely sure you fully understand what is being said, take the time to get clarification. It is worth the effort.
- Devote your full attention to anyone who is talking to you.

These tips are common-sense suggestions for being a better listener. They are not difficult, and they don't require special training. What they do require is the desire to be a better listener.

Listening to yourself also requires motivation, desire, dedication and determination. This is true because listening to yourself moves you from listening to action. If you truly listen to yourself and discuss your goals, your priorities for happiness and health, it follows as the night the day, there will be action. You will want to "make it happen."

Take time today to focus on listening to others AND to your own thoughts.

95

Every Four Years

It's not just about growing four years older.

A number of things happen every four years. Just think about some of them, because they seem to happen more frequently than every four years; we should be taking advantage of them as they happen.

One of these events is a leap year, in which February begins and ends on a Friday. In February 2008 there were five Fridays. Between the years 1904 and 2096, leap years that share the same day of the week for each date repeat only every 28 years.

What is a leap year? A leap year is a year in which one extra day has been inserted at the end of February. A leap year consists of 366 days. Did you know that there are three criteria for determining which years will be leap years?

1. Every year that is divisible by four is a leap year;
2. of those years, if it can be divided by 100, it is NOT a leap year, unless
3. the year is divisible by 400. Then it is a leap year.

According to the above criteria, the years 1800, 1900, 2200, 2300 and 2500 are NOT leap years, while years 2000 and 2400 are.

Another significant "every four years" event is the Olympic Games, which are subdivided into summer and winter sporting events. Up until 1992, both were held in the same year. The year of the summer games was, of course, 2008.

A little history about the Olympic Games: The original Olympic Games were first recorded in 776 BC in Olympia, Greece, and were celebrated until AD 393. The first modern international Olympic Games started in 1859.

Today the Olympic program consists of 35 different sports, 53 disciplines and more than 400 events. The Summer Olympics includes 28 sports with 38 disciplines; the Winter Olympics includes 7 sports with 15 disciplines.

Over the years, there have been many examples of outstanding achievement in the Olympics, as well as many heart-breaking events. The Olympics have had their share of drug-related problems, political situations, terrorism and violence, as well as controversy over amateurism and professionalism.

As spectators, we are able to enjoy the outstanding competition and, for the most part, excellent sportsmanship. We can share in the excitement and enthusiasm of record-breaking performances from athletes from all over the world.

Of course, we are for our athletes and want them to succeed, but I think it is fair to say that we Americans still do appreciate all athletes who are participating at their very best. It is much like world-wide family or friends competing together at the highest level possible as athletes, not as one race or one nationality against the other. We expect our American athletes to represent our country well and they do.

You can also say that a high percentage of Americans are fully behind our athletes and want only the very best for them and their families. We are together as we should be. No one is arguing about which state the athlete is from, or his or her race or religion, whether conservative or liberal or Republican or Democrat. We care only that they are Americans representing themselves and our country at the Olympics.

This is why so many people all over the world love the Olympic Games and, during the time of the Games, assume a different feeling about the people of the world. This is good. It should continue during the four years that follow until the next Summer Olympic Games to be held in London in 2012.

The next "every four years" event is the presidential election. This is a different story. Maybe we should all try to learn from our athletes and our participation in the Olympic Games. Why shouldn't both parties work in a sportsmanlike way to do what is best for our country and our people? Get rid of the politics and get with sportsmanship!

Encourage sportsmanship in more than just athletics.

96

CELEBRATING

My Favorite Things

It's important to do something.

When things are not going so well and for whatever reason you just feel down, what do you do to pick yourself up? If you are feeling sad, how do you get that happy feeling again? It's no fun to be down or to be sad, so what are some ways to brighten up the day and outlook on life.

One idea is to think about *The Sound of Music* and the song, "My Favorite Things":

> *When the dog bites,*
> *When the bee stings,*
> *When I'm feeling sad,*
> *I simply remember my favorite things,*
> *And then I don't feel so bad.*

In the song, Maria tells about some of her favorite things, such as raindrops on roses and whiskers on kittens, bright copper kettles, warm woolen mittens and brown paper packages tied up with strings. These are good lyrics for a song, but I don't think I would include them as some of my favorite things.

Granted, everyone would have different favorite things to think about. Men and women most likely will have different things on their favorite-things lists, which is understandable.

The point is that having a favorites list is a good idea. If one is feeling sad because of a dog bite, a bee sting or whatever reason, it really is good to have a "favorite things" list to remind us of those special, personal, favorite things.

Some that come to mind follow:

- A special event with the family
- A favorite poem—to read and maybe memorize again

- A favorite book—to read again and share with a friend
- A favorite movie that could be rented and enjoyed
- A favorite CD or music that does something for you
- A favorite friend whom you can visit or call
- A favorite event or accomplishment to remember
- A favorite passage in the Bible
- A favorite relative or friend who is no longer here, but of whom you have good memories
- A favorite meal, dessert or treat
- A favorite vacation to remember or scrapbook photos
- A favorite teacher

There are many favorite things to do that will make one happy and provide additional favorite things to remember in the future. These could include going shopping, planning a vacation trip, traveling, going to a ballgame, redecorating a room, planting a garden, helping a friend, spending time with family, playing golf, hiking, planning a dinner party, doing some charitable deed, or whatever brings you joy.

What is important is to do something. It is good to think about favorite things. It is probably better to DO favorite things, but why not do both. Think and do—remember and act!

 Write your list of "My Favorite Things."

97

Fourth Quarter

It's a great time for a Hail Mary pass.

When you hear someone talking about the 4th quarter, what comes to mind? Do you think about a football game or what? For sure, it means the last 4th of something. The 4th quarter follows three previous quarters. In football many games are won or lost in the 4th quarter of the game.

If you think about the best football games you have seen this year or in past years, the 4th quarter is probably what you remember most. How many have been won with a Hail Mary pass or some other spectacular play?

Do you know who first used the term, Hail Mary pass? It is believed to have been coined by Roger Staubach in referring to his desperation, game-winning touchdown pass to Drew Pearson in a 1974 NFC playoff game. In discussing the play during a post-game interview, Staubach told reporters that he closed his eyes, threw the ball as hard as he could, and said a Hail Mary prayer. Although the term may date further back, no reference has been cited as yet which predates Staubach's account.

Doug Flute's game-winning Hail Mary pass in 1984, with Boston College upsetting the University of Miami, is well remembered.

Why is the 4th quarter so important? Probably the best answer is that it is the last chance to win the game. It is the time to use all you have learned during the first three quarters to make adjustments and have a plan for success. This means knowing what needs to be done, taking action with the right calls and using time effectively.

In life we also have a 4th quarter each year which starts October 1 and runs until December 31. This is the time for making adjustments, having a plan for success, taking actions, making the right calls and using time effectively. It is the same as was mentioned about the 4th quarter in a football game.

How do we do this 4th quarter planning and analysis? First of all, recognize the value of getting started early in the 4th quarter. Don't wait until you only have time for a "Hail

Mary" to have a winning year. The odds for success are not good if there is procrastination until late in the quarter.

Some suggestions for the 4th quarter of this year:

- Find your New Year's resolutions or your list of goals and objectives for the year. Review them to see which ones have been completed and which ones still need attention.
- For the open items, rank them in an order of importance, which should be a reflection of your priorities.
- Decide which ones can be accomplished during the quarter and which ones will need to be carried over until next year.
- Start a list of goals and objectives for next year and include those carry-over items from this year. It is okay to add new ones at this time.
- Decide if any of the new goals and objectives could be started this year. What benefits would you receive from having a running start on next year?
- Give consideration to adding new actions for the quarter that might make this year even more successful than planned. As an example, increase chartable giving.
- Focus on the open action items that have been identified as top priorities.
- Plan to go into the holiday season with a positive attitude and be ahead of the game by actions taken early in the 4th quarter.

Know that there will be great satisfaction in having a strong finish with actions taken in the 4th quarter.

Plan to make the 4th quarter the best time of the year.

98

Take Your Time

"Fools rush in where angels fear to tread."

"Fools rush in where angels fear to tread," said Alexander Pope. How true this is. Not only fools, but all kinds of people rush in by acting and speaking too quickly. There is probably not a more accurate expression to describe saying something without thinking, or acting first before analyzing the consequences of the act. It really says it all, with the exception of not including a description of the possible outcomes.

The vision that we have of rushing in where angels fear to tread isn't a pretty picture. The expression generally means that something is going to happen that's not good, because angels would be wise enough to avoid the situation.

We had a salesman who was very knowledgeable, but he had a bad habit of interrupting customers when they were talking. He simply didn't listen. Consequently, he missed valuable opportunities and oftentimes ended up going where angels feared to tread.

So what does this mean to us?

I believe thinking about this well-known saying should act as a motivator for us to be more thoughtful and considerate. It should be a reminder to think before rushing into situations and to listen more carefully before talking.

The message is to take your time, but not too much. There is another saying that should go along with "Fools rush in where angels fear to tread": "He who hesitates is lost." This means that a person who spends too much time deliberating about what to do loses the chance to act altogether. This also happens often.

Put the two sayings together and the answer turns out to be to take the *right* amount of time to make decisions, to answer questions, to speak to others and to take actions. This makes sense, but what is the right amount of time?

The answer is that the right amount of time is different for almost everyone and for almost every situation. It should be a wake-up call for you if others are saying things like the following:

"Slow down—you're going too fast!"
"Sit down—you're rocking the boat!"
"A rolling stone gathers no moss."
"Why don't you take time to smell the roses?"

If these sound familiar, you probably are not taking the *right* amount of time to answer others' questions, take actions or make good decisions. These comments or similar ones indicate that it might be good to evaluate what you are doing.

Likewise, if you feel others are waiting on you for answers or your decisions, you might be taking too much time. If this is the case, you might be missing opportunities or the chance to act.

A wise person once said that if everything is under control, you're too slow. But, it wouldn't be an indication that you are taking the right amount of time if everything is out of control.

A suggestion would be to analyze each interaction with others from the perspective of an outsider, and rate yourself as too fast, too slow or just about right. Think also about the times when you moved too quickly. What was lost or what could have been accomplished better if you had taken more time for analysis? In those cases in which you felt you took too long, were opportunities lost?

This kind of informal analysis should be beneficial for both business and personal interactions. Another idea would be to talk to a good friend who would be honest with you. Ask him or her if you generally act too quickly or take too much time in making decisions or answering questions. If your analysis and their answer to your question are the same, it probably is accurate. Then you can decide what adjustments you want to make to become a better friend, leader, communicator or partner.

Focus on taking the right amount of time to make decisions and answer questions.

99

CAREER

To Be or Not to Be

Be proactive and positive.

"To be or not to be, that is the question." And a very good question it is. The phrase comes from William Shakespeare's *Hamlet,* which was written about 1600. It is one of the most famous quotations in world literature and the best-known of this particular play.

Many of us ask this question repeatedly during these difficult economic times. Maybe we use different words, but the questions we are struggling with are whether it would be wise (nobler in the mind) to take action or just to wait it out. These "be" questions for most people would have to do with investments, our government leadership, our job, our home and our family.

For example, to be or not to be in the market. Or to be or not to be supportive of our president's program. Other important questions: Should I be concerned about my job? Should I be doing something differently? Should I not be taking any special actions?

Did you ever hear the saying: "Leave a bee be and the bee will leave you be"? Obviously, this means don't mess around with bees because they will sting you. In business that same question can be asked.

In this case the bee would be your boss or your business. They are both "b" words so it is okay to use them. So, think about this: Is it possible that if you leave your boss be and continue as you have in the past, the boss will leave you **be**—meaning to **be** gone?

 If there is even a slight possibility of this happening, consider the first question: "To be or not to be, that is the question." If you seriously want to continue to be employed where you are, consider taking some or all of these "be" actions:

"Be" Action Tips

- Be proactive—Take actions to let your boss know you want to keep your job.
- Be positive—In these times, it is important to be an optimist and an encourager of others.

- Be an example-setter—This can be done by coming to work early and staying late, always completing assignments on time, asking good questions and going that extra mile.
- Be a team player—Support the others in your department and lift up those who need some special help or attention.
- Be a contributor—Make suggestions for saving money, increasing productivity, improving quality, focusing on customer satisfaction and eliminating waste in materials and labor.
- Be a company ambassador—Do this by communicating the good news about your company and the employees. Avoid rumors or negative discussions; turn them around whenever possible. It's true what your mother taught you: If you can't say something nice about someone, don't say anything.
- Be responsible—One way to be responsible is to believe this saying: "If it is to be, it is up to me."
- Be dependable—Say what you mean and mean what you say. If you agree to do something, do it. Do more than what is expected of you.
- Be a communicator—Communicate your ideas and concerns with your boss. Let him know that you and others in the company want to keep your jobs and are willing to be flexible in difficult times. This could mean accepting a different job, lower pay, shorter hours or any number of things that will keep the team employed and together.
- Be a leader—Focus on leading, not managing.

This is the time to **be** the best that you can **be.** The question remains: "To be or not to be, that is the question." The answer is a resounding *to be!*

Be all these "Be" things and more.

100

CELEBRATING

Sounds Like Christmas

It's more than music.

Yes, it's beginning to sound a lot like Christmas. This is the time of year when familiar sounds tell us Christmas is coming. These sounds can bring feelings of joy and anticipation or they can bring feelings of anxiety and sadness. Probably, as much as anything, it is our own thoughts and feelings that make us receptive to good thoughts or to worries as we hear these Christmas sounds.

Very familiar sounds are the Salvation Army volunteers ringing their bells outside of stores as we enter and when we leave. The ringing bell is to remind us that there are many who are in need, and even small donations by many people can be a big help.

Have you ever been a volunteer or watched as people and families come into close proximity of a Salvation Army bell-ringer? It is an experience, because it seems the people who are less able to give are the ones who are generous and happy about giving. So often the ones who look capable of contributing in a big way just walk by without even acknowledging the bell-ringer.

A few years ago, I volunteered to be a Salvation Army bell-ringer, as have so many people in our community. I experienced first-hand that so many joyfully gave and others, who obviously had the means to help, just walked by. This bothered me, so I tried ringing the bell louder when someone chose to pass up the opportunity to contribute. I think God taught me a lesson that day because as I was ringing loudly at one individual who was walking by, the bell broke and the ringer went sailing down the corridor of the mall. I was left without a bell to ring but with a lesson learned. I was not to judge anyone's contributing or not contributing. I didn't know anything about any of these people and I certainly hadn't walked in their shoes. It wasn't up to me to ring the bell louder at one person more than another.

When you think of the sounds of Christmas, you just have to include all the wonderful Christmas music you hear during this season. If asked your favorite Christmas songs, you probably would be like me and say it depends. It depends on the setting, the mood you are in, whom you are with and whether you feel like listening or singing.

No matter the mood, the setting or other circumstances, I'll bet the favorites will still be those traditional songs that have to do with the birth of Jesus: "Hark! The Herald Angels Sing," "Silent Night," "O Holy Night," "Oh Come All Ye Faithful," "O Little Town of Bethlehem," "Away in a Manger," "Joy to the World," "What Child Is This?" "The First Noel" and many others. Be sure to take time to enjoy these musical sounds to recall the real meaning of Christmas.

There are special sights and sounds associated with family traditions, such as watching a favorite Christmas movie. These wonderful old movies, such as *It's A Wonderful Life, Miracle on 34th Street, A Christmas Carol* and others, help to get us in the right Christmas spirit. Watching these movies with loved ones is time well spent.

Christmas wouldn't be Christmas without hearing the sounds of someone reading from the Bible. "In that region there were shepherds living in the fields, keeping watch over their flock by night. Then an angel of the Lord stood before them, and the glory of the Lord shone around them, and they were terrified. But the angel said to them, 'Do not be afraid; for see I am bringing you good news of great joy for all the people: to you is born this day in the city of David a Savior, who is the Messiah, the Lord. This will be a sign for you: you will find a child wrapped in bands of cloth and lying in a manger.' And suddenly there was with the angel a multitude of the heavenly host, praising God and saying, 'Glory to God in the highest heaven, and on earth peace among those whom he favors.'" (Luke chapter 2 verses 8:14)

The sound of the Christmas greetings, Merry Christmas, is important and real and must not be taken away from us in any way.

Yes, it's beginning to sound a lot like Christmas. Thanks be to God.

Wish others a Merry Christmas often.

101

CULTIVATE CHARACTER

Lessons Learned

Remember and take advantage of lessons learned.

When you move into the New Year, it's a good time to think about all the lessons that were learned last year. Take a few minutes to make a list of these lessons with descriptions.

The reason for putting the lessons learned in writing is so they can be remembered and used as a record for future reference. The main purpose for this little exercise is to learn from the lessons. Put your list in a very visible location, such as on the refrigerator door. Seeing the list on a regular basis will be a reminder of what you have learned and will help you to stay focused on your goals, which were developed from the lessons learned. This is the year to have constructive and positive results from what was learned last year. Start this today.

The question is, if there was a lesson learned, but no action taken, was the lesson actually learned? Or would it just be something we remembered or thought about but, for some reason or other, chose to ignore? Maybe the lesson was not important enough to us, or perhaps it just wasn't high enough on our list of priorities or plans for the year, to merit action.

Chances are, the lesson learned was important enough to deserve some kind of attention. If it weren't that important, you wouldn't be thinking about it in the first place. Perhaps your subconscious mind is helping you to use what you have learned over the past year.

For me, a good lesson learned this past year has to do with weight control. The lesson is not to blow all the good work done during the year trying to maintain the *right* weight by letting go over the holidays. If a lifestyle of accepting what to eat, the right quantity and the right amount of exercise works for ten months of the year, why do something different in November and December?

Why should the temptations be greater and the willpower weaker during this time of year? It doesn't make sense, because getting back to pre-holiday weight the first half of the New Year is much more difficult.

This is one of my lessons learned from last year and I intend to live up to the challenge this year. There—I said it and it is in writing!

Another lesson learned is to continue to "just do it." If there is a question of doing something or not, just do it. If it were not meant to be, you probably wouldn't be giving so much thought to whether or not to do it. I believe it always works, especially when it has to do with acts of kindness for others. Think about whether or not to visit someone who is in the hospital or home ill. Even if you just spend a few minutes visiting, you have shown you care and caring is certainly appreciated.

Communicating with friends and family more often is another lesson learned. Think how good you feel when you take the time to call an old friend whom you haven't seen or heard from for some time. If this makes you feel good, just imagine how the person being called feels. Sometimes a personal, hand-written note will have the same effect, so why not do both?

What are your lessons learned from last year? What actions do you feel should be taken this year to take advantage of this learning experience? Identify these lessons learned, put them in writing, decide what actions you want to take and then "just do it."

Take advantage of the lessons learned last year to make this a great year.

102

CULTIVATE CHARACTER

First Impressions Might Be Misleading

The wrong first impression could be your loss.

A picture is worth a thousand words. So is a first impression of a new acquaintance. If the impression is favorable, there will be a desire to continue the development of the relationship and get to know the individual better.

If the impression, for any number of reasons, is not favorable, however, it is quite likely that no more effort will be given to getting to know the other person. This would be a picture with a thousand words *not* read.

Some say a first impression is made within the first three seconds of a new encounter. This is when you are being evaluated or are doing the evaluation. In that short period of time, the evaluation usually puts the person being evaluated into one of three groups:

1. Comparable business or social status, and as such, would be considered acceptable for additional time together.
2. Higher status, so this person would be one who could be admired and developed as a valuable person to know.
3. Lower standing, so they might be completely ignored.

Grouping people like this can be a huge mistake, and the loser will be the one who chooses to live with what probably are incorrect and incomplete first impressions.

As an example, I was flying on an international fight on which the seats were close and the flights were long. I was assigned a center seat next to a woman who was not an outwardly attractive person. My first thought was not to enter into conversation with her. But, I always try to meet the person next to me on flights and learn something about them. Well, I did just that with this lady. It turned out she was a dean in charge of the department of surgery at a prestigious eastern medical school. She was brilliant and tremendously interesting. We had a great time together on this flight.

If I hadn't started this conversation, it would have been I who missed out on this experience.

Another time, while flying from Pittsburgh to Dallas, I was seated next to a very large young man who, because of his size, took a little extra room that I thought was mine. I was not happy about this and my first inclination was to just ignore him. Again, however, because of my commitment to get to know the person next to me, I started a conversation with him. He told me he was returning from Canton, Ohio, and had also spent a few days with his father in Pittsburgh.

I asked him if he had visited the Football Hall of Fame while in Canton. He said yes, and explained he was there because his father had just been inducted into the Hall of Fame. After the ceremony, he had spent a few days with him in Pittsburgh where his father was one of the Steelers' coaches. Turns out he was the son of Mean Joe Green and a very interesting and nice young man who was playing football for North Texas State, his father's alma mater.

Again—my gain. Both of these situations showed that just going by first impressions could be wrong. In addition, I wouldn't have been able to use either of them as examples of why you shouldn't rely on first impressions.

First impressions can determine future relationships or reasons why some relationships never get started.

I recently read a book about Dewey, a cat who lived in the library in Spencer, Iowa. This cat had the ability to find people in the library who needed special help or attention. Dewey would befriend, with tenderness and attention, both young and old who were having a difficult time in their lives.

I suppose Dewey had a cat's sixth sense for receiving real first impressions of visitors at the library.

During a recent college and fraternity reunion, I asked a college student who was transporting us around campus, where she was from. After telling us that she was from Spencer, I asked her if she knew Dewey, the library cat. She said yes, and added that Dewey had bitten her.

The purpose of sharing this story is to encourage you to think about the value of first impressions. Think about taking your time to form impressions, don't be catty and for sure don't bite new acquaintances. For if you do, someone might write about you.

Be very careful about making first impressions.

103

Birds of a Feather

You knew what I was when you picked me up.

This is not necessarily an article about politics. It also is not necessarily an article not about politics. Mostly it is an article about people—real people.

A friend of mine was discussing political candidates and said it reminded him of a story: "The Little Boy and the Rattlesnake." The story was about a rattlesnake that asked a little boy to take him up the mountain because he was old and dying and wanted to see the mountaintop before he died. The little boy said no, because he was a rattlesnake and would bite him and he would die. The snake promised he would not bite the little boy.

The boy took the snake up the mountain and returned him the next day to his home. When the snake was home, he bit the little boy. The little boy asked the snake why he had bitten him after he had promised he wouldn't. The rattlesnake looked up at him and grinned: "You knew what I was when you picked me up, and you should have known what I would do."

The point my friend was making was that we know who our politicians are. No matter what they say and how eloquent their speeches, we do know what most of them really stand for in their convictions. We can expect them to be the same when they are in office.

Thinking about the elections, business associates, personal friends, organizations, churches, classmates or any kind of relationship with others, a few old sayings come to mind that seem appropriate today.

It is said, "A leopard cannot change his spots and a tiger cannot change its stripes." In reference to people in general and politicians in particular, the leopard spots/tiger stripes reference is clear. They are who they are and they cannot change.

Another one: "Birds of a feather flock together." The meaning of this is also clear: Those of similar taste congregate in groups. You can tell a lot about someone by knowing his friends and associates. Likewise, knowing what organizations and church he or she belongs to and supports shows where the heart is.

"You can't judge a book by its cover." It's what's inside the book that counts. It is also what's inside people that is most important. Good appearance and the ability to speak well are assets that are valuable in both personal and business life. This, however, is only the cover. The book is about the individual's character, convictions, values and morals; they are the true measure of the worth of the individual. That is what counts.

"Judge not a man by his words, but by his actions." And "Actions speak louder than words." Mark Twain said, "Actions speak louder than words, but not nearly as often." We all want friends, associates and leaders whose actions, not their words, demonstrate who they are and where they are going.

Theodore Roosevelt said, "I have always been fond of the West African proverb 'Speak softly and carry a big stick; you will go far.'" This, along with Henry David Thoreau's "Rather than love, than money, than fame, give me truth." Oh, if we could just have our leaders or potential leaders listen to these few quotations from the past and believe in them—and follow them.

Pass on "birds of a feather" thoughts to others who might have serious concerns.

104

We the People

The government needs to be restrained.

The following is a quote from a newspaper article: "I think there's a general feeling we need to give serious attention to our monetary and budget problems; that perhaps foreign aid has been too big and we should give more attention to some problems within the United States. We need to give more attention to the development of industry and employment. This can be done by increasing the incentive for industry to expand by improving the tax situation."

This article was in the *Des Moines Register and Tribune* in 1963 and the author was listed as C.T. Bridgman, 54, in charge of engineering and research for Goodwin Companies. Chuck Bridgman was my father.

For some reason, this newspaper article just surfaced from one of the many stacks of "things" I have on my desk and surrounding areas. When I read it again after many years, it made me think about what we really want our government to do for us and what we personally want to do.

So much is being said about government's becoming bigger and having more controls over almost everything we do. This has been said many times in the past, and yet we just keep feeding the growth, probably mostly for political purposes.

I like what my Dad said back in 1963. "We need to give serious attention to our monetary and budget problems." We must put some controls on the government's excessive spending. "We need to give more attention to the development of industry and employment. This can be done by increasing the incentive for industry to expand by improving the tax situation." We know this works, so why not do it? We know we need to become more energy-independent, so why not do it?

Our government's being out of control has resulted in serious problems for our economy. This is not a political statement, because both parties are at fault for our present-day situation. These past weeks have led many of us to think about our own personal situations and future elections. It is a difficult time, because most people strongly feel the government needs to be fixed. It doesn't mean changing the basic government or our constitution; it means changing our politicians who aren't doing their job.

Patrick Henry said, "The Constitution is not an instrument for the government to restrain the people; it is an instrument for the people to restrain the government—lest it come to dominate our lives and interests."

The government does need to be restrained, but in a way that is consistent with our Constitution. It is our responsibility to communicate what the people want to our politicians in Washington; not for our politicians to communicate to the people what they want.

In business, a salesman represents the customer's interests and needs and communicates this back to headquarters. A really good salesman spends about the same amount of time and energy "selling" headquarters to take care of the customer as he or she actually spends with the customer face to face. When salesmen are transferred back to headquarters and are physically removed from the customers, it is interesting how quickly they become "headquarters" people. They tend to forget the importance of taking care of the customers.

I think this is also true with our politicians. When they were one of us, living with us, they knew what was important. Then they moved to Washington, became part of the "inside" group and quickly lost touch with us, our needs and what is important to us and our country. It is time to get them back on our side.

Be sure to support and vote for those candidates who you feel care about what is most important to you.

Vote and provide assistance to those who need help to vote.

105

New Year's Resolutions

The celebration of the New Year is the oldest of all holidays.

Don't you wonder how New Year's resolutions ever got started? Why should there be a specific time of year when we traditionally decide to do things differently? If this is important, why not do this on our birthday, or if it is a financial resolution, why not on April 15? If there is a real need to make changes in our lifestyle, shouldn't these changes start today?

Did you know the tradition of the New Year's resolutions goes all the way back to 153 BC? Janus, a mythical king of early Rome, was placed at the head of the calendar.

The Romans named the first month of the year after Janus, the god of beginning and the guardian of doors and entrances. He was always depicted with two faces, one on the front of his head and one on the back. Thus, he could look backward and forward at the same time.

At midnight on December 31, the Romans imagined Janus looking back at the old year and forward to the new. The Romans began a tradition of exchanging gifts on New Year's Eve by giving one another branches from sacred trees for good fortune. Later, nuts or coins imprinted with the god Janus became more common New Year's gifts.

Actually, the celebration of the New Year is the oldest of all holidays. It was first observed in ancient Babylon about 4,000 years ago. The Babylonian New Year celebration lasted for eleven days. Each day had its own particular mode of celebration. I guess you could say we are similar in a way, with college football bowl games starting December 20 and continuing until January 7.

During this ancient time period, the New Year was on March 25. There were problems with the calendar and the synchronization of the sun, so the Roman senate, in 153 BC, declared January 1 to be the beginning of the New Year. Other changes to the calendar took place during the following years. However, Julius Caesar, in 46 BC, firmly established January 1 as the New Year.

What all this means is that it would be safe to assume that, if you feel you want to make New Year's resolutions this year, you can plan on it being January 1. Nobody wants to mess around with Julius Caesar, so continue with the tradition of making New Year's resolutions begin on January 1 and to be forgotten by (you fill in the date).

If you don't feel like filling in the date, why not consider making plans and setting goals for this next year instead of resolutions? That way, you can plan for the whole year. You can be flexible; you can make changes. You can make plans and set goals for fun things. They don't have to be those old painful resolutions like losing weight, getting in shape and eating the right kinds of food.

Your plans could include spending more time with family and friends, enjoying life more, helping others and doing more random acts of kindness. While doing these more enjoyable things, you could also go ahead and lose some weight, start an exercise program and make wiser food choices.

I suppose having two faces, as did Janus, who could look forward and backward at the same time, would have certain benefits. Since we can have only one face at a time, however, I would rather have the forward-looking one. How about you?

 Make fun plans and goals for the year.

Great Service Comes from the Heart

Decide to make a difference.

Some stores have employees who seem to really care about the customers. Some restaurants have good food and provide outstanding, friendly service. Some companies have employees who seem to be naturally customer-focused, consistently doing the right things to satisfy customers. Unfortunately, there are many stores, restaurants and companies whose employees don't seem to care about the customers, don't give friendly service and are not customer-focused.

Why do some employees perform at high levels of customer care, while others don't seem to have a clue about providing service to the customers? There can be many answers to this question. Most answers would include the manager, whose job it is to get things done through employees. To do this, the manager should be able to motivate employees.

There have been many studies on employee motivation to determine what employees desire most from their jobs. It is interesting that most of these studies show that the number-one factor is job security. One of these studies shows the top job motivators:

- Job security
- Advancement opportunities
- Personal recognition
- Pride in the company for which they work
- Type of work

Pay and benefits were given low ratings, but they are very important, especially if the employees feel they are underpaid and the benefits are not reasonable.

There is an old saying that you can take a horse to water, but you cannot force it to drink; it will drink only if it's thirsty. This also is true of people. They will do what they want to do unless they are motivated in the right way with the right tools.

Barbara Glanz is a professional speaker who is recognized as an employee motivation expert. She has given many programs for hundreds of companies that want to motivate their employees. I heard about one of these in which she was working with a large grocery store chain.

She was telling her audience that all the employees at each grocery store could make a positive difference. She told them that the goal was to create memories so that customers would want to come back. When questioned how this could happen, her answer was to "put your personal signature on your job."

Several weeks after the meeting, a 19-year-old bagger named Johnny called Barbara. He told her proudly that he was a Down Syndrome child and hadn't known how he could make a difference since he was only a bagger. He told her that after much thought, he had come up with the idea of giving each of his customers a "thought for the day" note, which he would sign and say "thanks" for shopping there.

Each night Johnny would come home and look for a thought for the next day. If he couldn't find one he liked, he would just make one up. His father helped him put this on the computer, print it out and cut them into small cards to put in people's grocery bags.

A month later, the store manager called Barbara to tell her that Johnny had transformed their store. Customers were lining up for Johnny's lane and coming to the store more often to get his thought for the day.

The success at this store came from Johnny. Not because his idea was terribly creative or innovative, but because it came from his heart and the customers knew it. Johnny chose to make a difference. What he did was show that great service comes from the heart.

This is a good story and it's true. The idea of deciding to make a difference and to put your personal signature on your job doesn't have to be only about your job or about giving service to customers. It can and should be about everyday life. This is a good example of providing an environment where the employees are motivated to create their own personal signature on their jobs. Johnny's example became a catalyst for others in the store to contribute and it grew and grew and grew.

Johnny's "thought for the day" idea was successful because it came from the heart. Let's think about how we can do a similar "Johnny" thing in our lives that comes from the heart.

Plan to put your personal signature to good use.

107

Being Fair Is Not Always Easy in a Tough Economy

What must be done, must be done.

Is it fair to be fair? What kind of question is that and what does it mean? During these difficult economic times, many companies are struggling with reduced revenue and income. No matter how caring the company is toward the employees, there comes a time when some kind of reduction in the workforce should be made.

This reduction should be carried out only after management has reduced their income levels, bonus packages have been modified, overtime has been eliminated, manufacturing and other costs have been reduced and the sales force is doing all it can do to generate orders. To save the company, it may become necessary for the owner or management to take actions that, although prudent, are not pleasant.

Let's look at some thoughts on what is right and what is fair:

In 1961, Jack Welch became CEO of General Electric (GE) and immediately began implementing his philosophy and changing the face of the company. His leadership and ideas led GE to great success and earned him the honor of being named "Manager of the Century" by *Fortune Magazine* in 1999.

One of his most famous ideas had to do with the handling of underperforming employees. His idea was to purge the company annually of the bottom 10% of the staff. There were several advantages and some disadvantages in this action. Welch's system created three groups: the top 20%, the vital 70% and the bottom 10%. At the end of the year, the bottom 10% were purged from the company.

Meanwhile, the top 20% received bonuses for their hard work. This worked very well for GE because it motivated employees to work harder so as not to be in the bottom 10% and it rewarded the real performers in the top 20%. Everybody knew where they stood.

One of the real advantages of this ranking system was that it forced management to make decisions about employees each and every year. Many companies put off taking actions regarding unproductive employees. This didn't happen with GE in the days of Jack Welch. This also positioned GE to be in ready mode to take the right kind of actions when the economy slowed.

If a company hasn't been using Jack Welch's ranking system, how do they decide whom to let go if it is absolutely necessary to reduce the workforce? Or if you are an employee, how do you know where you stand?

The management and supervisors of the company can make recommendations based on the best workers and the worst. It is hard for supervisors to make this determination because it means one of their employees will be losing his or her job. It is difficult for a supervisor to be fair.

I was discussing this situation with the CEO of a local company, and he told me what he was doing to make this decision easier for the supervisors. He asks his managers and supervisors to answer one question about each of their workers: If the employee being evaluated had left the company and was applying to come back, would you rehire him or her? If the answer is no, that obviously tells you something about that employee.

For employees, why not look at this in a similar way? If you were no longer with the company and were looking for a job, would you want to return to your present company? If the answer is yes, then take the opportunity to tell your manager how you feel about your job and the company. If your answer is no, then it is up to you to see what you can do to contribute to your company, so that your answer becomes yes. If you can't figure out a way to get a yes answer, you might want to consider making a change when the time is right.

It is fair to be fair and kind to be kind in times such as we are experiencing. This should be a goal for all of us.

Focus on being fair and kind.

108

Move Up or Move Out

Shouldn't the non-performers be the first to go?

Some say they don't agree with Jack Welch's philosophy of terminating the bottom 10% of the work force each year. It seemed to work well for GE when he was CEO, and I'm sure a number of companies copied his management style in this and other ways. It is fair to say that Jack Welch was controversial, but GE's results under his leadership were not controversial—they were good.

Those who don't agree with Welch say it isn't right to terminate arbitrarily 10% of the work force each year. Some of those 10% might be good workers, they say. Others say this works only for large companies; maybe this is true to some extent.

If you follow the 10% rule and have 10 employees, you would have to let one employee go. If your company has 1,000 employees, you would have to let 100 go each year. Which is easier to do? This is a difficult question to answer. Let's look at this 10% "let go" policy from the perspective of both the company and the employee.

Think about those who are in the bottom 10%. Who would want to be in the lowest 10% of all workers at a company? What kind of job satisfaction would there be for these employees? How long would anyone want to live with this situation?

The bottom 10% are those employees who are not likely to get pay increases or be considered for advancement. They probably are not invited to go to off-site training programs or to enjoy other optional company perks. They are sort of the forgotten ones or the ones who are left behind. That is, until the business slows down and some employees have to be terminated. Then they become very visible, but not in a good way.

Wouldn't it be much fairer and kinder for the employees, and better for the company, to let the bottom 10% decide their future well before it's time to terminate them? The decision for the employees would be to take the actions necessary to develop their talents in order to move well above the bottom ranking, or transfer to different jobs where their abilities are better utilized. If these two options aren't available or possible, then the employees need to find jobs at different companies where their talents and experience are needed and will be appreciated.

On any athletic team, if 10% of the players are not performing well or are lacking in talent, chances are that team is not going to be great. As long as these players are on the team, the success of the team will continue to be limited. It is only when these players are traded or released and replaced with more talented or motivated players that the team will become better and more competitive. Even the very best players will perform at a higher level if the supporting players are doing a better job in their respective positions. The same is true for business operations.

You don't add more talented people to your organization if there aren't open positions. You have to create these openings in order to fill them. That means there has to be a plan to let the lowest-performing employees be replaced by higher-performing workers.

For these reasons and many others, it is good business management to care about all the employees, including the top performers, by taking action at the right time with the underperforming workers. This is why "Move Up or Move Out" makes sense.

Decide what makes good business sense for you.

109

Birthdays Hold a Special Place in Life

Think about the wish you make as you blow out your birthday candles.

Have you noticed lately that birthdays are coming around much more often? It seems that you just celebrate one, and in a very short period of time, someone is saying or singing "Happy Birthday to You."

This apparently rapid passage of time makes you think about birthdays in general. Why do we have them? How did this birthday recognition originally get started? Are the greeting-card companies responsible for making birthdays come around so fast?

It is difficult to know definitively the origins of many of our modern-day celebrations. This is true about celebrating birthdays. Some historians tell us that once people figured out how to tell, by studying the moon, when a year had passed, birthday celebrations began.

At that time, there was great thought and emphasis on superstition. These ancient people believed they were haunted and hunted by evil spirits. These spirits, according to legend, were especially strong when someone was going through a significant life event, such as getting married or even turning a year older.

This is why the tradition of having a party on one's birthday began. It was believed that, by having lots of friends and family around, by laughing and having a good time, the evil spirits would stay away.

It was also believed that loud noises scared off the evil spirits, which is why we have noise-makers and singing as part of our birthday celebrations. Blowing out candles and making a wish also had to do with both evil and good spirits. The flames sent a signal to the good spirits, and the smoke and fire somehow warded off the bad spirits.

On a birthday, especially with a birthday cake and candles, "Happy Birthday to You" is always sung. Everyone knows the words and many have added other music to complement this popular song. And popular it is. The 1998 *Guinness Book of World Records* says that "Happy Birthday to You" is the most recognized song in the English language.

What songs do you think follow the birthday song as most recognized? "For He's a Jolly Good Fellow" and "Auld Lang Syne."

The melody of "Happy Birthday to You" comes from "Good Morning to All," which was composed by American sisters Patty and Mildred Hill in 1893. A number of events followed the addition of "Happy Birthday" to the original song, which resulted in a copyright, owned eventually by the Time Warner Company, with royalties of more than $2 million per year.

So, does that mean singing "Happy Birthday" in public is copyright infringement? The answer is yes. The United States copyright law would lead you to believe that if you sing "Happy Birthday" to your family at home, you're probably not committing copyright infringement. If you sing it in a restaurant, however, it may be considered copyright infringement.

One of the most famous performances of "Happy Birthday to You" was Marilyn Monroe's rendition for President John F. Kennedy in 1962. There were many comments about Marilyn's song, but I'll bet not many questioned whether she had paid royalty on her performance.

The song was also sung by the crew of Apollo 9 on March 8, 1969. Royalty or no royalty, you just have to agree that singing "Happy Birthday" to someone you love is special and full of meaning.

The wish made while blowing out the candles is supposed to be known by only the birthday honoree. When I blow out the candles, I have a recurring wish. It is more like a do-over wish. You know what a do-over is. It would be the opportunity to do over something that happened in the past. When my sister and I were in college, we completely forgot about our father's birthday one year. Both of us forgot! I still feel bad about that and wish for a do-over to wish my dad a Happy Birthday.

Happy Birthday, Dad!

If you forgot someone's birthday in the past, make up for it this year.

110

Yankee Doodle Dandy

You can be patriotic by flying the flag, voting and supporting our troops.

As we approach Independence Day celebrations each year on July 4th, it is only natural for us to be thinking about being patriotic and doing patriotic things. What does this mean and how can we be patriotic or more patriotic?

Every citizen can be patriotic. Being an American and being patriotic mean different things to different people. I suppose this is because of life experiences, how we were brought up, our political inclinations and how our parents and influential teachers felt.

The following are a few actions that should be right for all American patriots:

- Fly the American flag—especially on Memorial Day, Flag Day, Fourth of July, Labor Day, Columbus Day and Veterans Day. Many fly their flags on other important holidays, such as Presidents' Day, Mother's Day, New Year's Day, Thanksgiving Day and Christmas Day.

- Register to vote—encourage others to register and vote in each and every election. Voting is a real sign of patriotism.

- Correspond with your congressional representatives and president. Let them know what you support and what you don't feel is right for our country. This does make a difference. It is not only your right to voice your opinion; it is your duty as a patriotic citizen of the United States.

- Show support for the soldiers who are fighting for our country. Sending mail or packages can mean a great deal to those who are away from home. So can helping families at home who have a loved one away fighting for our freedom. There are many needs for which help can be given and which will be appreciated greatly.

- Be of good spirits about our country and our heritage. A good way to do this is to think of the many patriotic songs that are so often sung on the Fourth of July. These seem to have a way of getting you in the right frame of mind for appreciation of America.

Don't you love to sing "I'm a Yankee Doodle Dandy" on July 4th? This song was written by George M. Cohan as a patriotic song for the Broadway musical *Little Johnny Jones*. The play opened at the Liberty Theater on November 7, 1904. It is about a fictional American jockey, Johnny Jones, who rides a horse named *Yankee Doodle* in the English Derby. That is why the chorus includes, *"Yankee Doodle came to London just to ride the ponies"*:

> *I'm a Yankee Doodle Dandy*
> *A Yankee Doodle, do or die*
> *A real live nephew of my Uncle Sam's*
> *Born on the Fourth of July*
> *I've got a Yankee Doodle sweetheart*
> *She's my Yankee Doodle joy*
> *Yankee Doodle came to London*
> *Just to ride the ponies*
> *I am a Yankee Doodle boy*

No matter what Mr. Cohan was thinking when he wrote these words, they are still great today. He had other highly motivational songs that showed the strong spirit and patriotism of the American and British people. Two well-known World War I songs were "Over There" and "It's a Long Way to Tipperary."

There is more to the story that you may or may not know. "Yankee Doodle" is a well-known British song, the origin of which dates back to the Seven Years' War.

The first verse and refrain, as often sung today:

> *Yankee Doodle went to town*
> *A-Riding on a pony;*
> *He stuck a feather in his cap,*
> *And called it macaroni.*

The song originated with a pre-Revolutionary War song performed by British military officers to mock the disheveled, disorganized colonial "Yankees." "Doodle" in the song means a fool or simpleton, and "macaroni" was slang for foppishness.

The Americans embraced the song and made it their own, turning it back on those who used it to mock them. This sounds so like our country—taking adversity and turning it into a positive motivator.

So, I like to think of being a "Yankee Doodle Dandy" and having a "Yankee Doodle sweetheart," which I surely do. For so many reasons, I am a lucky "Yankee Doodle Dandy" and so are you.

Have fun singing these old patriotic songs with loved ones.

Listen to the Quotes

Take comfort in remembering your favorite quotations.

Why do people read quotes? I think there are many reasons we are drawn to read them. Most people probably read them for enjoyment, entertainment and inspiration. Others simply are searching for just the right quotation to include in a talk they are preparing. In doing such a search, many new quotations are discovered and probably remembered for some future use or enjoyment.

When times are tough and things seem to be going in the wrong direction, I find comfort in remembering famous quotations from famous people. I wonder how these well-known people from the past could have been so wise. I also wonder why our politicians today can't be just as wise.

Politicians are quoted mainly for their inane statements or comments. At least sometimes there is humor in what they say, such as referring to "jobs" as a three-letter word.

I know there is much less being written today because so much of our communication is verbal—with or without a teleprompter. This might be the reason why there are fewer well-known quotations from people today than from those in the past. This might be true, but it doesn't explain why our politicians don't seem to be nearly as wise as our early political leaders.

As an example, Benjamin Franklin said, "He that goes a borrowing goes a sorrowing." Think about all the massive spending programs that our government is undertaking. The real sorrowing won't be felt by those doing all this spending—it will be felt by our children and their children. They are the ones who will be sorrowing and wondering what in the world we were thinking.

Alexander Pope said, "For fools rush in where angels fear to tread." It's too bad that this quotation fits so many situations today.

Benjamin Franklin also said, "God helps them that help themselves." Franklin didn't say God helps those who turn to the government for help. There is so much wisdom in this famous saying. I believe one of the most important reasons for our success as a country is that generations of Americans felt they had the opportunity and responsibility to help themselves. Unfortunately, this has changed over the years.

What hasn't changed over the years is our love and respect for the American Flag. The flag itself has only changed with the addition of stars. The original flag and our flag today consist of thirteen equal horizontal stripes of red (top and bottom) alternating with white; now we have fifty stars instead of the original thirteen.

There are many well-known quotations and songs about our flag that bring us feelings of joy and patriotism. Just think about these words from Henry Ward Beecher:

> *A thoughtful mind, when it sees a Nation's flag, sees not the flag only, but the Nation itself; and whatever may be its symbols, its insignia, he reads chiefly in the flag the Government, the principles, the truths, the history, which belongs to the Nation that sets it forth.*

People all over the world see our Nation and who we are when they see our flag. George M. Cohan gave us much to enjoy and remember, including "It's a Grand Ol' Flag."

> *You're a grand old flag*
> *You're a high flying flag*
> *And forever in peace may you wave.*
> *You're the emblem of*
> *The land I love*
> *The home of the free and the brave.*

Yes, we are the home of the free and the brave and a shinning example for other countries. With this comes the responsibility to provide encouragement and support for others who want freedom for their countries. We should be there.

It seems appropriate to close with a famous quotation from Abraham Lincoln:

> *You can fool some of the people all of the time, and all of the people some of the time, but you can not fool all of the people all of the time.*

We don't want to be fooled at all.

Send copies of your favorite quotations to your congressman.

Action Categories

Career
Actions that help to improve performance in order to become a more productive employee or manager; steps to take in finding employment.

Caring
Actions that emphasize concern and empathy for others.

Celebrating
Actions concerned with joy, remembrance, special occasions and holidays that are important events in our lives.

Coaching
Actions that stress leading, motivating, instructing and training in achieving goals or improving performance.

Committing
Actions that apply to completing tasks on time or taking a particular course of action for a specific objective.

Communicating
Actions that focus on a two-way process wherein listening is as important as speaking; guidance in written and oral communication.

Country
Actions that highlight our country's strengths and suggest areas for improvement; emphasis on patriotism.

Cultivate Character
Actions that focus on improving or strengthening moral or ethical character.

Index